FabJob

Become an Ice Cream Shop Owner

Barbara Lightner

FABJOB® GUIDE TO BECOME AN ICE CREAM SHOP OWNER
by Barbara Lightner

ISBN: 978-1-897286-55-5

Library and Archives Canada Cataloguing in Publication

Lightner, Barbara, 1953-
FabJob guide to become an ice cream shop owner / Barbara Lightner.

Also available in electronic format.
ISBN 978-1-897286-55-5

1. Ice cream parlors--Management. 2. New business enterprises.
I. FabJob II. Title. III. Title: Become an ice cream shop owner.

TX945.L54 2009 647.95068 C2009-905873-1

Important Disclaimer: Although every effort has been made to ensure this guide is free from errors, this publication is sold with the understanding that the authors, editors, and publisher are not responsible for the results of any action taken on the basis of information in this work, nor for any errors or omissions. The publishers, and the authors and editors, expressly disclaim all and any liability to any person, whether a purchaser of this publication or not, in respect of anything and of the consequences of anything done or omitted to be done by any such person in reliance, whether whole or partial, upon the whole or any part of the contents of this publication. If expert advice is required, services of a competent professional person should be sought.

About the Websites Mentioned in this Guide: Although we aim to provide the information you need within the guide, we have also included a number of websites because readers have told us they appreciate knowing about sources of additional information. (**TIP:** Don't include a period at the end of a web address when you type it into your browser.) Due to the constant development of the Internet, websites can change. Any websites mentioned in this guide are included for the convenience of readers only. We are not responsible for the content of any sites except FabJob.com.

FabJob Inc.
19 Horizon View Court
Calgary, Alberta, Canada T3Z 3M5

FabJob Inc.
4616 25th Avenue NE, #224
Seattle, Washington, USA 98105

To order books in bulk, phone 403-949-2039
To arrange a media interview, phone 403-949-4980

www.FabJob.com
THE DREAM CAREER EXPERTS

Contents

About the Author

Barbara Lightner is an experienced researcher and writer who specializes in reference and educational publications. She has worked in a variety of careers and says "I believe that each of these careers has helped to shape me and proven beneficial in each subsequent career."

As a teacher in the 1980s, career exploration was a focus of her Language Arts program. She later had the opportunity to write and edit articles for two editions of the *Encyclopedia of Career and Vocational Guidance,* and copy edited numerous books in Ferguson's Careers in Focus series as well as its *Career Resource Guide for People with Disabilities*. She has worked for World Book Publishing since 1989, fact checking articles in the *World Book Encyclopedia* and for other publications.

Lightner lives near Chicago, IL, and is an avid outdoor enthusiast who likes to hike and swim in her spare time.

Acknowledgements

Thank you to the following experts and organizations (listed alphabetically) for generously sharing insider information and business advice in this FabJob guide. Opinions expressed in this guide are those of the author or editors and not necessarily those of experts interviewed for this guide.

- *Gary Bales*
  President, Carvel Corporation, Atlanta, Georgia
  www.carvel.com

- *Katie Dolan Dix*
  Owner, Capannari Ice Cream, Mount Prospect, Illinois
  Director, National Ice Cream Retailers Association
  www.capannaris.com

- *Irene Macones*
  Longtime Carvel franchisee, West Paterson, New Jersey

- *Pam Nardinelli*
  Owner, Marble Slab Creamery, Woodland, California
  www.marbleslab.com

- *Aaron Serruya*
  Co-founder, Yogen Fruz, Toronto, Ontario, Canada
  www.yogenfruz.com

1. Introduction

Congratulations on taking the first step towards starting your own ice cream shop. It's a step into the fast-paced, challenging world of food retail. A step into a place where people love to go when they have a craving for something tasty and special; where contributing to people's joy as they treat themselves to special indulgences and special moments is all part of the service.

Chances are you've been in dozens of ice cream shops and you might possibly have worked in one or two. While it can be fun and rewarding to work in someone else's shop, nothing quite compares to the satisfaction of running your own business and taking credit for your own ideas and flashes of brilliant customer service.

The *FabJob Guide to Become an Ice Cream Shop Owner* was put together to help you realize your dream of becoming a business owner in this exciting industry. In this guide you'll find everything you'll need to succeed, from learning about the skills you'll need and where to develop skills you may lack, to start-up budget planning, to finding financing for your new venture.

First, let's take a look at the growth trends in the ice cream and frozen desserts industry. In the rest of this chapter we'll examine what it's like to operate an ice cream shop by taking a look at the environment you'll be working in. We'll show you what a typical day is like for an ice cream shop owner. Then, we'll outline some of the many benefits of being an ice cream shop owner.

1.1 A Growth Industry

As you start out in your new business, have confidence that you will be part of a well-established and ever-growing market. Ice cream sales are a $23 billion industry in the United States, according to the International Ice Cream Association, and a significant amount of that ice cream is purchased at ice cream shops. According to the International Dairy Foods Association, Americans spent $13.9 billion on ice cream purchases eaten away from home in 2006. Canadians are also big ice cream consumers, spending nearly $2 billion on ice cream and frozen desserts in 2005, according to Agriculture and Agri-Food Canada.

A Recession-Proof Business

Sales of ice cream at ice cream shops tend to be strong despite any economic fluctuations. Due to their relatively low price, ice cream and other frozen dessert products are somewhat recession-proof and may even benefit during economic downturns. For example, people who might be reluctant to eat out at a fine dining establishment may increase their ice cream purchases as a way to satisfy their desire for eating out and indulging in something special.

Consumer Preferences

The ice cream and frozen desserts industry is huge and includes a wide variety of products. These are:

- Low/non/fat, regular, premium, and super-premium ice cream
- Soft serve ice cream
- Hard frozen yogurt and soft frozen yogurt
- Sorbets
- Gelato
- Frozen ices
- Ice cream novelties, such as ice cream bars and ice cream cakes

Americans annually consume nearly 14 quarts per person at ice cream shops and other establishments that sell frozen desserts. Soft ice cream makes up the largest segment of these purchases, each person annually eating an average of 4.6 quarts, followed by hard ice cream (4.5 quarts), frozen novelties (3.0 quarts), soft frozen yogurt (1.2 quarts), hard frozen yogurt (0.2 quarts), and other miscellaneous frozen items (0.4 quarts).

Consumer preferences in Canada parallel those in the United States with consumers eating 9.2 liters of ice cream a year, according to Agriculture and Agri-Food Canada. Unlike the United States, however, frozen yogurt makes up a greater share of all products sold (4%) and has shown sales gains of 12% between 2000 and 2005.

Ice Cream in a Health-Conscious Age

You might be nervous about opening an ice cream shop in our modern, health-conscious society. However, you can take comfort in knowing that, despite a growing interest in low-carb foods among health-conscious and weight-watching North Americans, many people are willing to forgo the low-carb, low-calorie products and consume the richer, creamier ice creams.

Consumers are also attracted to higher quality ice creams, such as those found at many specialty ice cream shops. In the early 2000s, for example, regular ice cream declined in sales in response to a growing consumer preference for super-premium ice cream. Although regular ice cream sales have since rebounded, consumer preference for specialty, gourmet, and super-premium products remains high. Many people consider ice cream an indulgence or special treat and they want the tastiest, fullest-flavored ice cream.

"We've seen a tremendous increased interest in nutritional and healthy foods in North America, and this wave is reflective of what's happening in most markets around the world. With the strong disposable income that baby boomers possess, they are constantly looking for 'better for you' alternative foods that will enhance their everyday lifestyle."

— Aaron Serruya, cofounder of Yogen Fruz

Increasing Popularity

In fact, your timing couldn't be better for opening your new shop. In the past decade, specialty ice cream shops and unique eateries are growing in popularity and replacing the traditional ice cream parlors as the destination of choice for ice cream lovers of all ages. Some of the fastest growing ice cream chains are those catering to consumer preferences for upscale and gourmet items. In addition to selling ice cream products, these stores sell the ideas of luxury and indulgence.

Great Moments in U.S. Ice Cream History

1776	The first ice cream shop opens in New York City
1812	First Lady Dolly Madison serves ice cream at President Madison's second inaugural ball
1851	Jacob Fussell of Boston becomes one of the first large-scale ice cream producers
1874	Soda fountain shops and soda jerks appear with the invention of the ice cream soda
1890s	The ice cream sundae is introduced
1946	Americans celebrate the end of World War II by eating 20 quarts of ice cream per person that year
1978	Ben and Jerry open their first homemade ice cream scoop shop in a renovated gas station in Burlington, Vermont
1984	President Ronald Reagan designates July as "National Ice Cream Month"; he names the 3rd Sunday in July "National Ice Cream Day"

Keep in mind that ice cream trends can be very volatile and can change rapidly. One example is frozen yogurt, which enjoyed immense popularity in the 1970s and 1980s, then nosedived to the point where it became extremely difficult to find a frozen yogurt shop. After approximately 20 years of lower popularity, frozen yogurt shops began to proliferate in select areas of the United States, such as California, and are now surging in popularity once more. As an ice cream shop owner, you'll need to be aware of growing trends and know when a trend has flattened or started to decline. Later in this guide we'll show you a number of resources that can help you stay on top of the trends.

1.2 Owning an Ice Cream Shop

As an ice cream shop owner, your job will be to satisfy your customers' desires for tasty, frozen treats. Many of your customers will come to your ice cream shop to celebrate, whether for a big celebration such as winning a soccer game or a small one such as getting a good grade on a test. Other customers will come just to indulge and treat themselves. All of these customers have one thing in common—they want to enjoy themselves and their ice cream treats.

Some ice cream shops offer an entertaining atmosphere with singing employees and "bells and whistles," while others emphasize quick service and the option to eat on site or take their purchases away. In Chapter 3, we'll look more in-depth at the types of ice cream shops you can open. In this section, we'll look briefly at some of the products you can sell in your shop and some of the services you can offer in addition to the frozen treats you'll be selling.

1.2.1 Products

As we mentioned previously, you can sell a wide variety of products in your ice cream shop. You can specialize in one product area, such as high-quality, premium ice creams that you create the recipes for and make on site, or you can sell soft serve ice cream, or frozen yogurt products. Perhaps your own tastes and experience draw you to gelatos or sherbets. Read on to learn more about the wide variety of products you can choose to sell.

Ice Creams

Types of Ice Cream

Ice cream comes in a range of products. Different grades of ice cream are classified according to government regulations that dictate the ingredients, especially the milk fats content. In addition, the various grades then become the basis for a huge assortment of different types of specialty ice cream, such as organic, exotic, ethnic, and so on.

There are several different grades of ice cream, classified according to the fat content in the formulation. The higher the percentage of milk fats (abbreviated mf, also called butter fat or bf) in the ice cream, the higher the grade. The lowest grade is "economy", which contains the legal minimum by which it can be classified as ice cream, around 10%. Anything below the 10% legal minimum is classified as a "low fat", "reduced fat", "non fat" or "light" product. (Previously, these were labeled as "ice milk" products.) This is followed by "standard" ice cream at 10%-12% mf, premium at 12%-15% mf, and super premium ice cream containing 15%-18% milk fats (although the maximum is usually around 16%).

A higher percentage of milk fats gives ice cream a creamier and richer taste. Today, standard and premium ice creams make up the largest share of the ice cream segment, although these have steadily been losing ground to super-premium ice creams.

Organic or All-Natural Ice Cream

Organic ice cream is a super-premium ice cream that caters to the growing trend for healthy and natural foods without additives or other artificial ingredients. In many cases, an entrepreneur first creates homemade organic ice cream and then opens up a shop to sell the product. Such shops are not necessarily small or restricted to a local region, either. One of the best known organic ice cream shops is Ben & Jerry's, which began selling homemade organic ice cream in 1978.

Exotic and Ethnic Ice Cream

Exotic and ethnic ice creams are a fast-growing trend. Ice cream makers add nontraditional spices and ingredients to super-premium ice cream to create unique flavors. Some shops choose to carry a few exotic flavors—such as ice cream made with West Indian fruit, which is popular in Miami or corn ice cream and pickle ice cream, both of which are popular in the Southwest and among people who enjoy Mexican food. Other multicultural favorite flavors include jack fruit, figs, purple yam, guava, avocado, buco, durian, green tea, lychee, papaya and passion fruit.

Some exotic flavors are not related to any specific ethnic cuisine but are the products of their creators' imaginations. Ice cream makers have used some unusual ingredients such as wine, herbs, and spices like white pepper to whip up batches of ice cream. One ice cream maker even uses lobster meat in its ice cream (see "Lobster ice cream? Get the scoop on the latest flavors" at **www.msnbc.msn.com/id/25679074/**).

Other Frozen Desserts

Soft Serve Ice Cream

Often considered frozen custard, soft serve is ice cream with a high quantity of air. This allows it to be dispensed from a machine and flow directly into a cone. Now served in both fast-food outlets and ice cream shops, some of the earliest retailers include Dairy Queen and Carvel. In 2006, sales of soft serve ice cream surpassed those of hard ice cream, making it the most popular category of all frozen desserts.

Frozen Custard

Custard-style ice cream, sometimes called French ice cream, is a cold dessert similar to ice cream. It contains a minimum of 10 percent milk fats, cream, egg yolk, and sugar. Although frozen custard is not sold by as many retailers as ice cream, it is popular in parts of Canada and the United States. Frozen custard stands and shops can be found in the Midwest, Southwest, and some Eastern states.

Frozen Yogurt

Frozen yogurt is a frozen dessert similar to ice cream. Made of yogurt, it is a low-fat or fat-free alternative to ice cream, and can be mixed with a variety of fruit and other flavors. Many manufacturers of frozen yogurt tout the health benefits of their products, but to be classified as a true yogurt, the product must contain live-culture bacteria. The National Yogurt Association provides the official Live and Active seal of approval to makers of frozen yogurt products.

Gelato

Gelato is Italian ice cream made of milk, eggs, sugar, and flavorings such as nuts, fruits, teas, and liquors. It has a low air content, resulting in a dense and rich-tasting product. Unlike super-premium ice cream, it has a low milk fats content (between 5–8 percent), resulting in a lower-fat product without sacrificing the taste. It is super-cooled during the manufacturing process and ideally stored in a cold air convection freezer, then served in a semi-frozen state.

Other Products

Other frozen desserts include flavored shaved ice and smoothies, sherbets (or sorbets), and blended drinks. Many shops also sell ancillary products, such as confectionary items, bakery goods such as pastries, or other snacks. Items often sold along with ice creams and frozen desserts include hot dogs, pizza, popcorn, coffee and iced coffees, chocolates, and nuts.

1.2.2 Services

As an ice cream shop owner you don't have to limit yourself to just selling ice cream. You can also offer services such as decorating and selling ice cream cakes, off-site catering services, and hosting birthday and other parties in your shop.

Birthday and Other Parties

If you have the room and facilities for it, you might consider hosting birthday parties and other parties in your shop. The best option would be to have a space separate from your main selling area where partygoers can celebrate undisturbed. If you already serve some of the other products mentioned in the previous section, such as hot dogs and pizza, you will be ready to host kids' birthdays, sports team celebrations, and just about any other kind of informal party people may want to celebrate at your establishment. Many of the in-house catering possibilities are the same as those you can offer for off-site catering as discussed below.

Catering

Many ice cream shops offer catering services in addition to their on-site offerings. While some do offer full-service catering (supplying all the food for the event), most provide only ice cream, frozen desserts, novelties and snacks like popcorn. Services offered can take the form of hand-scooped ice cream service, ice cream cart rentals fully stocked with ice cream and novelties, or even sundae bars featuring a make-your-own sundae service. Some of the events that ice cream caterers service are:

- Anniversaries
- Birthdays
- Business meetings
- Casual Fridays
- Christmas parties
- Company celebrations
- Company picnics
- Graduations
- Grand openings
- Groundbreaking ceremonies
- Health and fitness fairs
- Ice cream socials
- New product rollouts
- Pool parties
- Tenant appreciation parties

To learn more about adding catering services to your service offerings, see section 3.1.

Ice Cream Cakes

Another service area to consider is creating ice cream cakes and decorating cakes. Cake decorating is a huge market, and most people appreciate the variety and novelty offered by an assortment of ice cream cakes. Ice cream cakes are sold in the same forms as other cakes (round, sheet, logs, and cupcakes). Ice cream pies are another option. Some of the many possibilities for breaking into the cake decorating and selling market include:

- Birthdays
- Holidays
- Graduations
- Baby showers
- Bridal showers
- Bar and Bat Mitzvahs
- Anniversaries
- Company parties and product launches

To get an idea of cakes offered by other ice cream companies, have a look at the websites of Baskin Robbins (**www.baskinrobbins.com/CCreator/cakecreator.aspx**) or Carvel (**www.carvel.com/products/cakes_pies.htm**). You can also take a look at Capannari Ice Cream's ice cream cakes and pies at **www.capannaris.com/products/cakes_and_pies**.

1.3 Benefits of Being an Ice Cream Shop Owner

Owning an ice cream shop can be a fulfilling and rewarding career. In addition to the benefits of working for yourself, it offers the possibility to shape the size of your business according to your own preferences and personal ambitions. You can work to establish a store that turns a profit and provides a fair income or choose to expand beyond the original store and open up another store once the first becomes profitable.

Fun Work Environment

What could be more fun than working in an ice cream shop? You'll feel like a kid again every time you step into your store. All the many varieties of ice cream to choose from, right there at your fingertips, and it's all yours.

No more 9-to-5 job, no more grumpy boss looking over your shoulder. When you're the owner of an ice cream shop, you'll set your own hours.

Many ice cream shops are a family affair, too. Imagine being able to spend time with your spouse and kids who can work right alongside you and learn the business with you. You'll also have the opportunity to work with many other young people and help them develop skills that will benefit them for years to come.

> *"The most rewarding aspect of being an ice cream shop owner is being able to do business with my family and friends around me all the time. When I was in the corporate world I worked away from everyone and by day's end there really wasn't much time left to enjoy family. With my family and I doing business together we get to spend more time around each other."*
>
> — Irene Macones, longtime Carvel franchisee

And the parties. You'll be an important part of helping people successfully celebrate events like birthdays, sports victories, and just about anything else that people want to commemorate by throwing a fun party. Every celebration will center on your unique ice cream and service offerings.

A Lucrative Business

Ice cream shops can be extremely lucrative. According to the U.S. Census Bureau, 68% of year-round shops have annual sales in the $100,000 to $499,999 range, with an additional 12% making upwards to $1,00,000. The Bureau of Labor Statistics reports that average gross profits range between 21 – 23 percent of sales, which translates into anywhere from $21,000 to $115,000 in potential earnings for you. Stores with high volume and low overhead costs often turn a profit within the first year.

Make People Happy

Most ice cream shop owners take great pleasure in helping make other people happy. They enjoy developing relationships with their customers and other members of the community, getting involved in community activities, and becoming respected members of the business community. And they get these benefits on a daily basis. You'll see the smiles and happy faces of customers from the very first day you open your doors for business.

Exercise Your Creativity

If you're a creative person, and you probably are, you can use your creative imagination in many different ways as an ice cream shop owner. Imagine developing exciting new ice cream flavors, undiscovered taste combinations that make your product list unique from other shops like yours.

You can also create a unique environment for people to enjoy your one-of-a-kind products. Many ice cream shops hearken back to long ago times by turning their shops into old-fashioned ice cream parlors or soda shops. If you remember the days of soda jerks or just long for a time when the neighborhood ice cream parlor was a center of activity on a lazy Sunday afternoon, you'll love owning your own ice cream shop.

Other ice cream shops make themselves focal points for fun by offering fun activities and events. You'll enjoy thinking up new ways to entertain people, perhaps making your customers sing for ice cream like Show Place Ice Cream Parlor in Beach Haven, New Jersey (**www.surflight.org/showplace.htm**), rated among the top ten ice cream shops in the entire U.S. Wherever your imagination takes you, you can realize your dream when you own your own ice cream shop.

1.4 Inside This Guide

The *FabJob Guide to Become an Ice Cream Shop Owner* is organized to help take you step-by-step through the basics you will need to open and operate your own store. The chapters are organized as follows:

Chapter 2 ("Getting Ready") explains the skills you will need as an ice cream shop owner and how to learn them.

Chapter 3 ("Starting Your Ice Cream Shop") will help you decide what kind of store you should open. This chapter discusses different products you can sell and will help you decide whether to buy an existing store, operate a franchise, or open a new store. It also explains what you need to get started, including your business plan, start-up financing, store name, and other important matters.

Chapter 4 ("Setting Up Your Ice Cream Shop") offers the information you need to actually set up your store. It gives advice on how to choose a location, design your store, and create inviting window displays. You will also discover where to purchase the equipment and supplies you will need.

Chapter 5 ("Running Your Business") takes you into the day-to-day challenge of running your store once it's open. It explains how to develop procedures and product manuals, and covers inventory management, financial management and pricing, marketing your business, and working with staff and customers.

Chapter 6 ("Getting and Keeping Customers") tells you ways to build up your customer base and how to keep your customers happy so they keep coming back. It describes ways to promote your shop through advertising, press releases, a website, and other promotional tools. It describes quality customer service—and how to ensure you are providing it.

By following the steps in this guide, you will be well on your way to living your dream — opening your own successful ice cream shop.

2. Getting Ready

One of the biggest attractions to owning an ice cream shop is that no formal education is required. Entrepreneurs can get started without investing extensive time or costly resources in retraining or schooling. But there are ways to educate yourself about the career so you can identify whether it is one that you really one to pursue and to learn the skills necessary to succeed in it once you become an ice cream shop owner.

2.1 Skills You Will Need

Do you have the personality and aptitude to become an ice cream shop owner? If you like to work with other people and enjoy helping others have a good time, this career may be for you. If working in a quiet room by yourself is more your working style, you may want to think twice about this career—unless you want to hire people to perform all of the ice cream shop's operations. Take the following self-evaluation quiz to discover if you have the natural aptitude to become an ice cream shop owner.

2.1.1 Self-Evaluation Quiz

Below are some questions that reflect traits shared by many ice cream shop owners. Make a mental note or put a checkmark next to all that are a "yes" for you.

1. ___ Do you enjoy people?
2. ___ Do you like making people happy?
3. ___ Do you like to work in a fun environment?
4. ___ Are you willing to work long hours, weekends, and holidays?
5. ___ Do you like to stay busy?
6. ___ Are you capable of multitasking?
7. ___ Do you work well under stress?
8. ___ Are you comfortable being on your feet for hours at a time?
9. ___ Do you love ice cream and frozen desserts?
10. ___ Do you enjoy entertaining people?
11. ___ When you're craving something special, is ice cream one of the first foods that comes to mind?
12. ___ When you travel, do you love to stop in ice cream shops?
13. ___ You see an ice cream shop and think, "I've got to bring my kids (or husband, or best friend) here. They would love this place."
14. ___ Do you almost automatically rate new flavors you sample as a "good seller" or a "no-go"?
15. ___ Do you consider yourself an entrepreneur?

These 15 questions offer insight into characteristics typical of individuals who enter and succeed in the world of ice cream shop ownership. How did you do? If you answered "yes" to all of these questions, you already have qualities found in successful shop owners. If you answered "no" more than you answered "yes", you may need to develop some of your skills a bit further, but that's what this guide is for. You'll find all the tools you'll need to become a successful ice cream shop owner later in this guide.

As we mentioned earlier, the skills you need to succeed as an ice cream shop owner can be learned. So let's take a look at the specific skills that can help you succeed in owning an ice cream shop. Later in this chapter you'll find plenty of resources to develop these skills through education and self-study.

2.1.2 People Skills

For most people, buying an ice cream cone at an ice cream shop is a different experience than picking up a quart of ice cream and a box of cones at a grocery store. Visiting the ice cream shop involves not only the actual treat but also the eating experience. A happy customer is more likely to purchase at your shop, become a regular customer, and tell others about your business.

There are a number of interpersonal skills that can help you develop excellent relationships with your customers — and your employees, suppliers, landlord, banker, and everyone else you do business with. This section offers some tips on how to enhance those skills. The sections that follow have tips for specific situations.

> *"The personal attribute that has most helped me to make a success of my store is my personality with customers. You can never have a bad day in the eyes of a customer. This is their down time and they are treating themselves to your product."*
>
> — Irene Macones, longtime Carvel franchisee

Listening

While listening seems like an easy skill to master, most of us experience challenges in at least one of the following areas involved in listening: paying attention, understanding, and remembering.

Are You A Good Listener?

Sometimes my mind wanders while the other person is speaking.	❑ Yes	❑ No
When someone asks me to do something, sometimes I forget what they've said.	❑ Yes	❑ No
If I do not understand what someone says, sometimes I nod my head and pretend like I do anyway.	❑ Yes	❑ No
I interrupt people sometimes, even when I do not mean to.	❑ Yes	❑ No
I jump to many different topics not always related to the topic at hand.	❑ Yes	❑ No

If you answered yes to more than two of the statements above, then you might want to work on your listening skills. You can become a better listener by focusing fully on someone when they are speaking. Here are some ways to do that:

- Don't interrupt the other person. Hear them out.
- Keep listening to the other person, even if you think you know what they will say next. If you make assumptions, you may miss the point they're making.
- Ask questions in order to clarify what the other person has said. Take notes if necessary.
- Don't be distracted by outside interference. Loud noises, the other person mispronouncing a word, or even an uncomfortable room temperature can break your concentration and distract you from the conversation.
- Give feedback to the other person. Nod occasionally; say things like "I see," and smile, if appropriate. Let them know you're listening.
- Use paraphrasing. In other words, repeat back in your own words your understanding of what the other person has said. It can help alleviate misunderstandings later on.

Verbal Skills

Clear communication is essential because you will need to explain your store's sales or return policy, and you will need to describe to customers your current inventory. When making sales, customers can become frustrated if they find it difficult to understand what you're saying. To improve your verbal communication skills, ask friends or a vocal coach for feedback on any areas that could be improved, such as: use of slang, proper grammar, or altering your tone of voice to eliminate any harshness. (You can find vocal coaches in the Yellow Pages.)

Reading Non-Verbal Messages

In addition to hearing what people say, a skilled business owner also notices non-verbal communication (tone of voice, facial expression, body language, etc.). These signals can give you valuable clues about what the other person is thinking.

For example, did a customer fold their arms when you made a particular suggestion? If so, they may be communicating that they disagree, even if they don't actually say so. Although body language can't tell you precisely what someone is thinking, it can give you clues so you can ask follow-up questions, even as basic as "How do you feel about that?" If you want to improve this skill, you can find some excellent advice in the book *Reading People,* by Jo-Ellan Dimitrius and Mark Mazzarella.

2.1.3 Business Skills

To succeed as an ice cream shop owner, you will need to effectively use a variety of business skills including:

- Business planning
- Financial management
- Merchandising
- Operations management
- Inventory management
- Hiring and supervising employees
- Marketing and sales

Experience you have in other retail environments can be helpful, and there are a number of ways you can develop your skills and knowledge in all of these areas. In this chapter, you'll find specific ideas to help you increase your experience and knowledge of running an ice cream shop. You'll also find detailed advice throughout the remaining sections of this guide.

You will probably find reading the entire guide before you launch your business helpful, but you can quickly identify particular areas you may want to focus on by reviewing the table of contents. For example, section 5.4 provides advice on financial management, covering everything from budgeting to bookkeeping to building wealth, and section 3.5 gives you advice about start-up financial planning. Both these sections provide website links to online resources to help you find further help in these areas.

One tool for helping you to focus on what business skills are involved in being a business owner is business planning. Section 3.4 looks in detail at how to develop a business plan to get your business up and running by outlining and clarifying what your shop will offer, deciding how you will finance your business, creating a market plan, etc. In addition to addressing these important business issues, a business plan will also help you to understand some of the other basic "hard" skills required of a business owner, such as marketing and accounting skills.

Canada Business (**www.canadabusiness.ca**, click on "Starting a Business") has a great deal of helpful information for anyone thinking of starting their own business. They offer the following tips to new entrepreneurs for identifying and creating a unique service:

- Take advantage of a market switch
- Capitalize on a growth trend
- Take advantage of new fads
- Cover market gaps or shortages
- Imitate a successful product or idea
- Transfer a concept from one industry to another

- Invent a new product or service
- Create a market demand
- Serve unique client groups
- Take advantage of circumstances
- Find people with under-used skills

As you can see from this list there are a great number of ways that you can make your business or services unique. For example, capitalizing on a growth trend, most ice cream owners now offer mainly super premium and specialty ice creams. This sets them apart from the supermarket fast food frozen dessert offerings, and helps them to create a special niche market.

Additional information on all aspects of starting a business is available through the following resources:

SBA

The Small Business Administration (SBA) is a leading U.S. government resource for information about licensing, taxes, and starting a small business. You can find a range of resources including information on financing your new business, business plans and much more at **www.sba.gov**.

SCORE

The Service Corps of Retired Executives (SCORE) is an organization of U.S. volunteers who donate their time and expertise to new business owners. You can find information on taxes, tips for starting your business, or even find a mentor who will coach you and help you maximize your chances of succeeding as a new business owner. Visit them at **www.score.org**.

Canada Business Service Centers

This Canadian government website offers information on legislation, taxes, incorporation, and other issues of interest to Canadian business owners or those who do business in Canada. For more information and a list of services they offer visit their website at **www.canadabusiness.ca**.

The National Restaurant Association

As the leading association for the restaurant industry, the National Restaurant Association offers valuable business resources geared specifically toward owners of food establishments. Its website at **http://restaurant.org** offers information on food trends, industry forecasts, running a business, and advice on getting started.

2.1.4 Ice Cream Making Skills

You don't necessarily need to know how to make ice cream or other frozen desserts in order to be successful as an ice cream shop owner. However, many shops in specialty niches such "old-fashioned ice cream parlors" and "ethnic" shops offer for sale unique ice cream products they manufacture themselves. If you're planning to purchase all your ice creams and other frozen desserts ready-made from a supplier, you can skip this section, although the information here can help you to better understand the process of ice cream manufacture.

Many ice cream shops offer their own home-made (also called artisan, handcrafted, or gourmet) ice cream. Selling ice cream and other frozen desserts that you make yourself on premises can be one way to make your ice cream shop stand out above your competitors. If you've thought about offering your own unique ice cream flavors you'll need to understand the process.

Making Ice Cream

As explained in section 1.2.1, there are ranges of ice cream quality based on the overall milk (or butter) fat content. This varies from 10% to about 16% depending on whether the ice cream is standard, premium or super premium. Anything less than 10% milk fat is classified as a low-fat product. In fact, there are strict government regulations (see section 3.6.5) governing ice cream labeling based on these ranges.

Essentially, ice cream is a frozen mixture of pasteurized milk, cream or butter, water, sugar, other solids, and flavoring. Generally, it has an air content of about 45-50%. Gelato is denser and contains 35% or less air, while soft serve ice cream can contain as much as 60% air.

The Process

Ice cream making is a fairly simple process. Even if you have never made ice cream you will have no trouble understanding how it works. Where it gets complicated is in calculating the milk or butter fat and other content of your recipe.

In the past, ice cream was made by mixing the ingredients in a container and then inserting it inside a second, larger container. The second container was filled with layers of ice and salt from bottom to top, completely surrounding the first container with the ice cream mixture in it. Then the first container was rotated (churned) by hand until its contents solidified.

These days, the process is even simpler. Most modern, mechanical ice cream makers come with a liner containing a special gel that is pre-frozen and then the container with the ice cream mixture is inserted into that. Again, the inside container is rotated, but using a motor instead of hand cranking, until the mixture solidifies. That's it. The process works the same way for other frozen desserts like gelato. (To learn more about commercial ice cream equipment you can buy for your ice cream shop see the section below.)

Calculating Milk Fat Content

An important consideration in making ice cream (or gelato, frozen yogurt and other frozen desserts) for sale is that you follow government guidelines for commercial ice cream production. (See the government regulations in section 3.6.5) Especially important is following the guidelines regarding milk or butter fats percentage and percent solids non-fat (percent solids non-fat is the sugar, gelatin, flavorings, etc. contained in the mixture), since these determine the labeling of your product (non-fat, low-fat, premium, etc.).

Milk fat (or butter fat) can be supplied to the mixture using either cream or butter. (Don't forget in your calculations that cream also adds water to the mix.) For comparison, butter is 80% fat, whole pasteurized milk contains 3.25% butterfat, half-and-half (the kind you use in your coffee) about 10-18%, and whipping cream 30% or more.

Solids non-fat (SNF) can be supplied by any of the following:

- Condensed skim milk (also adds water)
- Condensed milk (adds both water and fat)
- Skim milk powder (adds small quantity of water)
- Sugar (sucrose or corn syrup solids)
- Sweetened condensed milk (adds water and sugar)
- Whey powder (also adds a small quantity of water)

To calculate how much of each ingredient you'll need to produce 10 lbs of ice cream, you first need to calculate the fat content. If you want to produce a super premium ice cream containing 16% fat and 30% solids non-fat, then the calculation is:

(10 x 0.16) ÷ 0.8 (fat content of butter at 80%) = 2 pounds of butter

So you would need 2 lbs of butter in order to add 16% butter fat content to your 10 lbs of ice cream mix.

To calculate the solids non-fat, the equation is:

10 x 0.30 = 3 pounds of condensed milk,
skim milk powder, sugar, etc., total weight

The amount of water required is calculated as the remaining weight after all the other ingredients are accounted for. So if you add 2 lbs of butter and 1 pound of sugar, skim milk powder, etc., then the weight of water would be 5 lbs (about 2.5 quarts).

Obviously, this is a very simplified look at these calculations. For example, the solid non-fats formula above doesn't take into account the amount of SNF contributed by the butter added. However, this does give you a quick look at what's involved in producing a commercial mix that follows government regulations. To learn more about this, you might consider taking one of the courses listed in section 2.5.2.

Overruns

An overrun is the increase in volume to the ice cream mix due to the addition of air as the mix is processed. An increase in volume from 1 gallon to 1.5 gallons as a result of air addition is a 50% overrun. The smallest overruns are in products such as super premium ice cream and gelato because these have much less air in them. The highest overruns are in soft serve ice cream, which, as mentioned earlier, can be as much as 60% air. If you wanted to produce 2 gallons of soft serve, your initial mix would only be about 1 gallon.

If you would like to read more about this subject on your own, one excellent and very detailed resource is the University of Guelph's Ice Cream pages at **www.foodsci.uoguelph.ca/dairyedu/icecream.html**. You might also be interested in the article "Soft serve ice cream: What's in there anyway?" available at **www.nationalpost.com/life/story.html?id=680377**.

Quantities to Make

How much ice cream you make to sell depends on several factors. First, you will need to consider how much of a given flavor you will sell in a certain time period. If you will be making more conventional flavors like vanilla and chocolate, you can probably count on these being mainstays and you will sell regular quantities. From your weekly or monthly sales you will be able to figure out how much you need on hand.

Commercial ice cream makers can produce a 3-quart batch of ice cream in about 20 minutes, and some much more than that. Of course, the ice cream will still need to be frozen for about 10 hours after that in order to harden it, but clearly you can produce and sell a batch of your ice cream in less than 12 hours. You can easily produce extra batches of your most popular flavors ahead of time and keep them in frozen storage so that you'll always have enough on hand.

Adding Flavorings

The flavorings you can add are limited only by your imagination. These days, people are trying out all kinds of weird and wonderful ice cream flavors. If you're developing your own recipes, you'll have to experiment with when to add the flavorings to mix. Sometimes these are added at different stages of the process. You may have to heat some ingredients and add them early on, or you might add other ingredients, like nuts or chocolate chips, near the end of the churning process but before the mix has completely solidified.

If you would like to read more about ice cream and other frozen dessert recipes one good online resource is **www.ice-cream-recipes.com**. Although it's not a commercial resource, the site features hundreds of recipes, including standards like vanilla and chocolate and more exotic flavors such as cinnamon and spice, pumpkin, avocado, prune, and so on. This site also features videos about making ice cream.

2.2 Learning by Doing

Active observation and participation in an ice cream shop may be the best way to learn about this career. Following are several suggestions for ways to learn more about ice cream shops.

2.2.1 Work in an Ice Cream Shop

Several of the ice cream shop owners we spoke with said they had originally worked for another shop. This can be a valuable way to learn much-needed skills for running your own shop one day. Not only will you learn how to deal with customers, you will more than likely learn how to use the systems used by many ice cream shop (covered in Chapter 5 of this guide).

Working in an ice cream shop (or in a restaurant or fast-food store), even if only on a part-time or volunteer basis, is probably the best way to prepare yourself for opening your own store. Working for a time in a ice cream shop will give you valuable insight into pricing merchandise, what sells (and, equally important, what doesn't), how to deal with customers, how to arrange merchandise to its best advantage so that it looks attractive to buyers, and exactly what it takes to keep a store running smoothly on a day-to-day basis.

As time goes by you will also find out where the owner obtains most of the inventory. This information will help when you're ready to open your own shop. Remember, if you do land a job in an ice cream shop, do not steal the owner's menu or any recipes. You might feel tempted to take this information and use it in your own shop, but it is likely to start you off in your own business with a sullied reputation.

Visit the shop you'd like to work in as a customer whenever possible before applying for a job so you can get to know the owner (and the shop) a little. Remember, it will help if the owner recognizes you because you have been there before. Never phone or write a letter; face to face works much better. Here are some suggestions for introducing yourself and what you can do for a prospective employer:

- Explain that you are interested in learning retailing.
- Tell them if you've had any previous selling experience (whether it's selling shoes or ice cream).
- Think of some extra service you could offer, such as creating product display boards.
- If no job is available and you really love the shop and want to work there, volunteer to work for free. It could pay in the long run.

Finally, when applying for a job in an ice cream shop ensure that your demeanor, personality and dress reflect the qualities that you would be looking for in an employee. These characteristics are outlined in more detail in section 5.5.2, "Recruiting Staff".

> **TIP:** Positions available in ice cream shops may be rare during the winter months, but almost any retail experience is valuable so apply to other food service establishments if you can't find a job at an ice cream shop.

2.2.2 Getting Related Food Service Experience

Caterers

As we mentioned earlier, many ice cream shops offer a variety of catering services. Working with a caterer can be an excellent way to learn more about this side of the industry. Whether you get any ice cream service experience or not doesn't matter. You'll get an inside view of the logistics of providing catering services.

To find catering jobs you can look in your local newspaper's classified ads or visit one of the food service specialty job boards listed below. Try search categories like "catering", "servers", "concessions", or "general help". You can also try sites like Monster.com, Jobster, or Yahoo! HotJobs using similar search terms.

- *Food Industry Jobs*
  www.foodindustryjobs.com

- *FoodService.com*
  www.foodservice.com/employment

- *H Careers Canada*
  www.hcareers.ca

Party Planners and Event Planners

To get experience in planning and executing parties, such as birthdays and other celebratory events, you might consider working for a party planning company. Party planners help their clients decide on themes, set party budgets, provide supplies such as food, beverages, decorations, etc., then supervise the event from start to finish. Some party planners work solo, although many hire part-time or occasional staff to assist them.

To find party planners who might be willing to hire you or let you volunteer your services to them, visit **www.partypop.com/Categories/Party_Event_Coordinators.html**. This site has a directory of thousands of party planners across the U.S. and Canada. You can also try the International Society of Events Specialists directory at **www.ises.com/ClientsandPublic/tabid/84/Default.aspx** to find event planners across North America.

2.2.3 Get Volunteer Experience

In addition to volunteering to your services to party and event planners, there are other ways to find volunteer opportunities to help you learn more about food service. For example, many ice cream shops sell ice cream at special events and community festivals. Volunteering to help man a booth can provide valuable insights about ice cream retailing in a very short time frame. Plus, you may pick up some tips for your own shop on how to promote and market your business.

You can find your local Conventions and Visitors Bureau at the Chamber of Commerce website the United States Directory of Local Chambers of Commerce & Visitor Bureaus website at **www.2chambers.com** (click on the link to the Convention and Visitors Bureau for your state). Check out your local Visitors Bureau "Events" page and look for events and festivals that might offer volunteer opportunities.

Service organizations such as the Rotary Club, Kiwanis, and Lion's Club sponsor events that often include ice cream service. Many of the programs they offer are geared toward children, and they are happy to accept volunteers to work at such events. Check with your local service clubs to see if they sponsor any events in which you can get some ice cream or food service experience as a volunteer.

Other organizations offering volunteer opportunities in ice cream or food service include zoos, hospitals, sports arenas, church events, local fairs, etc. Many communities have volunteer bureaus whose websites you can check for volunteer opportunities.

Here's an example of a volunteer opportunity for working in an old fashioned ice cream parlor from Luther Manor (**https://luthermanor.org/volunteers.asp**), a retirement care facility in Wauwatosa, Wisconsin:

ICE CREAM PARLOR SERVER

Serve frosty treats and conversation to residents and guests. Volunteer in an old fashioned ice cream parlor. Friendly, outgoing personality. Comfortable with money exchange. Good customer service skills. Shifts available 7 days a week, from 1:30-4:30 p.m. Tuesday/Thursday, and Saturday, 8:45-11:15 a.m.

2.3 Be Your Own "Mystery Shopper"

You have probably heard of mystery shopping, where companies hire people to go into their various retail outlets and pose as shoppers. This is an excellent way for management to get feedback about what their retailers are doing wrong — and right. In order to take a first-hand look at how other people are running their own ice cream shops, you can become your own mystery shopper using these tips. You will find this information particularly helpful as you put together your business plan (see section 3.4) and marketing plans (section 6.1).

To begin, take a look in your local Yellow Pages under categories such as ice cream and frozen desserts. Select a variety of types of shops, such as old-fashioned ice cream parlors, scoop shops in malls, and independently owned and franchised stores. Take time to visit several shops that interest you.

As you go to a number of stores and record your observations, a couple of things will begin to happen. First, you will begin to know what stores are in your area and which, if any, will be competition for you. Second, you will get a chance to see stores in action. There is no substitute for seeing first hand how ice cream shops really run and operate.

Take a small notebook and pen so you can discretely take notes. After you have been to each store, use a Store Impressions Form like the one on the pages that follow to record your observations.

TIP: As you assess local stores, remember that what you see there should simply serve as ideas. There are no hard and fast rules about what your own store must carry.

Store Impressions Form

The Storefront

1. Is the shop easy to spot from the street? ❑ Y ❑ N
2. Is it easy to park? ❑ Y ❑ N
3. Is there plenty of free parking or street parking? ❑ Y ❑ N
4. Is it an area with foot traffic? ❑ Y ❑ N
5. How is the area? ❑ Y ❑ N
6. What kinds of people do you see on the street? ❑ Y ❑ N

Entering the Shop

1. What do you notice about the atmosphere?
2. What do you like about the way the shop looks?
3. What do you notice about the physical layout of the shop?
4. Does the shop seem inviting or uninviting? Why?
5. Is the shop clean? ❑ Y ❑ N
6. Do you think you could get to a section you were looking for without assistance? ❑ Y ❑ N

The Staff

1. Are you greeted? ❑ Y ❑ N
2. Does the staff seem:

Welcoming?	❑ Y ❑ N	Indifferent?	❑ Y ❑ N
Pleasant?	❑ Y ❑ N	Pushy?	❑ Y ❑ N
Impatient?	❑ Y ❑ N		

3. When you ask a question, how do they respond?
4. Are they knowledgeable? ❑ Y ❑ N
5. Are you able to get your questions answered to your satisfaction? ❑ Y ❑ N
6. Does the staff make you feel comfortable about asking a question? ❑ Y ❑ N

Using the Shop

1. Can you browse the selections easily? ❑ Y ❑ N
2. Do you feel rushed to order? ❑ Y ❑ N
3. Are you comfortable? ❑ Y ❑ N
4. Is seating available and comfortable? ❑ Y ❑ N
5. Are the restrooms easily accessible and clean? ❑ Y ❑ N
6. How is the lighting?

Merchandising

1. How are the food products arranged?
2. What is the quality of these products?

3. Do the products seem priced according to their quality? If not, why not?

Food Preparation Areas and Service Area Displays

1. Was the food preparation area functional for staff? ❑ Y ❑ N
2. Was the food preparation area clean? ❑ Y ❑ N
3. Was the text on the display board visible and easy to read? ❑ Y ❑ N
4. Are photos of the product shown on display board or wall posters? ❑ Y ❑ N

Buying

1. Is the cash area organized? ❑ Y ❑ N
2. Is it easy to get served? ❑ Y ❑ N
3. Are there long lines of people? ❑ Y ❑ N
4. Does the staff member speak pleasantly to you? ❑ Y ❑ N
5. Were you offered a sample? ❑ Y ❑ N
6. Did you buy anything? ❑ Y ❑ N

   Why or why not?

Leaving

1. What are your impressions when you leave?
2. Does a staff member notice you are leaving? ❑ Y ❑ N
3. Does anyone thank you? ❑ Y ❑ N
4. Does anyone say goodbye to you? ❑ Y ❑ N
5. Do you feel positive about your experience? ❑ Y ❑ N

Overall Impressions of the Store

1. What did you like most about the shop?

2. What did you like the least?

3. What did you notice about the store's logo, bags or other printed material?

4. Will you go back to the store in the future? ❑ Y ❑ N
5. Will you recommend this store to anyone? ❑ Y ❑ N

In addition to observing anonymously, getting an ice cream shop owner's permission to let you observe them in action is also a wonderful way to learn. If you have a friend or a business contact that will let you spend a day seeing how they operate their business, it will be an excellent learning experience.

2.4 Learn From Other Business Owners

2.4.1 Talk to Ice Cream Shop Owners

After speaking with dozens of store owners, we recommend approaching ice cream shop owners via e-mail, through an organization of business owners, or by driving to a non-competing store and asking their advice.

The ice cream shop owners we spoke with were eager to offer advice and point out many additional resources. A good way to find other ice cream shop owners is to check your Yellow Pages or Google "Ice cream directory" and the city or region you are interested in.

If you can get a store owner to talk to you, you can learn an amazing amount of insider information from someone who could be doing just what you want to do. Keep in mind, however, that while some may be quite willing to talk, others may be too busy. But if you ask nicely for information many people are very glad to share it.

> **TIP:** You will probably have a hard time if you approach a store owner who could be considered your direct competition. There is a difference between sharing knowledge and giving away trade secrets. Make sure that the experts you try to contact are not your direct competition.

So, how do you contact ice cream shop owners? Try the following steps:

- Identify first what it is you are trying to accomplish
- Make a list of questions you want to ask
- Identify who you think you should talk to

- Make a list of contacts
- Take the steps to make contact (email, telephone, in person)

For example, let's assume you went to a great ice cream shop in a neighboring town. First (after you have made your list of questions), find out the phone number and the owner's name. Then call and ask to speak to the owner.

Here is a sample phone script:

> *"Hi, I am Kara Cream. I was in your store while I was on vacation and I really enjoyed it. Could you tell me who the owner is? (After you are connected to the owner, Ima Infogiver, you proceed.)*
>
> *"Hi, Ima Infogiver? My name is Kara Cream and I am considering opening an ice cream shop in another part of the state. I was on vacation and had a chance to stop in your store, and I loved it. (Now, ask permission to ask — an old sales trick.) I was wondering if you would be willing to let me ask you a couple questions about how you do things. I could use some expert advice."*

TIP: It never hurts to tell experts you think they are experts. Most people like being recognized for their accomplishments.

Make an appointment to call back the store owner at their convenience. Then take some time and decide on a couple of questions you really want answers to. Ask only these questions. Also, offer to correspond with your contact using email if the expert prefers this. Always thank the expert for their time and make sure they know you appreciate the information. If you build this relationship slowly you can ask for more help and advice, and perhaps you can even find a mentor.

Remember to:

- Ask permission to ask questions
- Be sensitive to the expert's time
- Decide ahead of time what you will ask
- Don't overwhelm your expert with too many questions
- Build the relationship slowly and ask for more time at a later date

As you do research on the Internet, you will undoubtedly begin to see ice cream store websites that interest you. All of these sites have contact information you can use to directly ask for help and advice.

Remember to adhere to the same advice in email that you would use on the phone. Be courteous, brief, and grateful. Don't worry if you have to send out a number of letters before you have a response. Ice cream shop owners are busy people. If you are polite and persistent, some store owners will be willing to talk to you.

As another option, consider turning to VocationVacations, a company that can set you up with an opportunity to test-drive a job you are interested in. For a fee of about $1,000 you get to experience the career hands-on as you work one-on-one with a mentor for two days. Vocation Vacations currently offers an Ice Cream Shop Owner opportunity. Visit them at **http://vocationvacations.com/search/results.php?category=Ice+Cream+Shop+Owner** (or from the home page click on the "Career Mentorships" link and then the "Dream Job Vacations" link and look for the job title mentioned above).

2.4.2 Join an Association

Industry Associations

To learn more about the retail ice cream industry, consider joining an association. Membership provides opportunities to exchange information with other ice cream shop owners and people in the industry, access to publications, and resources, and other benefits.

National and regional industry associations for owners of ice cream shops include the following:

National Ice Cream Retailers Association (NICRA)

Members of this trade organization include retail ice cream shop owners throughout the United States, Canada, and many other countries. The association helps new shop owners get started and provides the opportunity for members to exchange ideas and information. Membership benefits include a monthly bulletin, annual convention, Ideas Folder, scholarship program, training videotape/DVD, contests, awards, and an ice cream clinic. The annual fee is $225. Membership information is available at **www.nicra.org/benefits.html**.

National Frozen and Refrigerated Foods Association (NFFA)

This association works to promote refrigerated and frozen food and represents retailers as well as wholesalers, manufacturers, distributors, and suppliers in all frozen and refrigerated food categories. It offers resources for promotional ideas as well as industry contests and promotional activities. Their website is at **www.nfraweb.org**.

Great Lakes Ice Cream & Fast Food Association (GLIC&FFA)

This association serves ice cream, yogurt, and fast food businesses. It offers educational seminars, a memberships kit, a newsletter, group insurance, and a scholarship to members' employees. Information on how to join and details on benefits is available at **www.glicffa.com**.

New England Ice Cream Restaurant Association (NEICRA)

Serving all of the states in New England as well as New York, New Jersey, and Pennsylvania, the primary purpose of this association is facilitating the exchange of information. It hosts an annual convention and publishes a tri-yearly newsletter. The annual membership fee is $100. Membership information is available at **www.neicra.org/join.htm**.

Other Associations

National Restaurant Association

This is the leading association in the restaurant industry and provides valuable information about industry news and trends, legislation, and related issues. It offers members an Information Service and Library, access to industry research, access to health and safety experts and a staff attorney, training, health insurance, property and casualty insurance, online job boards, and credit-card processing services, among other benefits. Membership fees vary by state. For more information and to learn how to join, go to **www.restaurant.org/join/**.

- *Ice Cream Alliance (U.K.)*
  Lots of information for retailers.
  www.ice-cream.org

- *International Association of Ice Cream Vendors*
  This association serves the needs of ice cream truck business owners.
  www.iaicv.org

Canadian Associations

Canadian Restaurant & Foodservices Association (CRFA)

This association tracks the industry and offers valuable business tools and publications, including industry reports and forecasts, start-up kits, free subscriptions to Restaurant News, and an online Buyers Guide. To learn more about membership and to check out its resources, visit the site at **www.crfa.ca/default.asp**.

British Columbia Restaurant & Foodservices Association (BCRFA)

The foremost industry association in British Columbia, BCRFA offers advocacy and valuable resources. For more information and to learn about membership benefits, go to **www.bcrfa.com**.

Canadian Association of Foodservice Professionals (CAFP)

This association serves the development of restaurant professionals. To learn more about its programs and membership, go to **www.cafp.com/default.asp**.

Once you're an established store owner, it's a good idea to join a national or regional association because membership gives customers confidence to see the Association's logo displayed in your place of business. Another benefit is the networking that takes place.

Business Organizations

You can also join a number of excellent organizations designed for business owners to learn and network in an organized setting. One excellent resource is your local Chamber of Commerce. Chambers usually have an annual fee and are set up to aid the local businessperson with a variety of business-related issues. Members attend local meetings and can also take part in events designed to help them be more successful.

To find out how to contact your local chamber, visit the national websites. For the U.S. Chamber of Commerce visit **www.uschamber.com**. For the Canadian Chamber of Commerce Directory visit **www.chamber.ca/index.php/en/links/C57**.

2.5 Educational Programs

2.5.1 Business Courses

Taking business courses is not necessary to run an ice cream shop. There are many successful business owners who are self-taught and have never studied business. Others have taken a course here and there but do not possess a degree. However, the skills you learn in business classes can come in handy. Check into the courses offered at your local community college, university, or business school.

To get some accreditation in business studies, consider taking a small business or bookkeeping program that will help you to better run your business. Most community colleges offer classes in these subjects and you will find the extra business knowledge very useful when you do get your store in operation. Depending on which of your skills you would like to develop, consider taking courses on topics such as:

- Advertising
- Basic Accounting
- Business Communications
- Business Management
- Marketing
- Retailing

If you are not interested in attending courses at a school, or you don't have the time, another option that can easily fit into your schedule is distance learning. Traditionally these were called correspondence courses and the lessons were mailed back and forth between student and instructor. Today, with the help of the Internet, there are many online courses available. Again, check your local community college, university, or business school to see if they offer online courses.

Your local Chamber of Commerce may also offer training courses and seminars for new business owners. Many also offer consultations with retired executives and business owners who are well-qualified to offer advice. Visit **www.chamberofcommerce.com** or **www.chamber.ca** to find a Chamber near you.

2.5.2 Ice Cream Workshops and Courses

While teaching yourself can be an inexpensive and fun way to learn about the retail ice cream industry, you may prefer to learn about ice cream and business operations from experts by signing up for an educational program. Although there are no formal programs required to qualify as an ice cream shop owner, there are a number of institutions offering training programs, extension courses and ice cream workshops designed primarily for those in the ice cream industry or people considering joining it.

SmallDairy.com gathers information on course offerings throughout the year and posts course titles, locations, sponsoring university or institution and links on its website at **www.smalldairy.com/courses.html#other**. This list may not be comprehensive, so be sure to check the following resources as well if you do not see them listed. The following list includes several of the most renowned university programs in the United States:

Penn State

Penn State's College of Agricultural Sciences offers two courses every year. The Ice Cream Short Course is a 7-day course described on Penn State's website as "the oldest, best-known, and largest educational program dealing with the science and technology of ice cream." Ice Cream 101: Introduction to Frozen Desserts is for ice cream lovers, ice cream shop owners, potential ice cream shop owners, and anyone interested in the small-scale manufacturing of ice cream. Both courses are offered annually in January, when many ice cream shops are closed. Agenda, fee, and registration information is available at **http://conferences.cas.psu.edu** or **www.creamery.psu.edu/ShortCourse.htm**.

University of Wisconsin

University of Wisconsin–Madison's College of Agricultural and Life Sciences offers a 3-day Ice Cream Makers Short Course. For more information, see **www.cdr.wisc.edu/shortcourses/pdf/ice_cream_09.pdf**. It also offers the Batch Freezer Short Course in March of every year. Designed primarily for manufacturers of frozen desserts who use batch freezers, the course provides hands-on practice in ice-cream making. Additional information is available at **http://dairyfoods.wisc.edu/batch1.htm**.

Cal Poly

Cal Poly's Dairy Products Technology Center offers ice cream professionals its Frozen Dairy Desserts Manufacturing Short Course every year. For more information, check its Continuing Education course offering at **www.calpoly.edu/~dptc/short.html#**.

University of Florida

The University of Florida–Gainesville and the University of Wisconsin–Madison collaborate to offer two extension workshops: Successful Ice Cream Retailing and Fundamentals of Batch Freezing. Courses are taught by ice cream retailers and university professors of food science, and are held in Gainesville, Florida and Madison, Wisconsin. For more information, go to **www.successfulicecreamretailing.com/index.html**.

University of Guelph (Canada)

University of Guelph's Department of Food Science offers a week-long Ice Cream Technology Course every year. The course is aimed at small-scale ice cream manufacturers, ice cream suppliers, and ice cream shop owners, retailers, and chefs who want to learn the technical aspects of ice cream production. For more information, visit its website at **www.foodsci.uoguelph.ca/dairyedu/iccourse.html**.

You can also find classes through commercial ice cream organizations, such as the following:

- Gelato & Pastry Institute of America offers 2- and 3-day seminars in Nevada and New York for ice cream shop owners and individuals considering opening a gelateria and adding it to their menu. Cost is $600 for the 2-day seminar and $750 for the 3-day seminar. Full program information is available at **www.gpiamerica.org/courses.htm**.

- Tharp & Young "On Ice Cream" offers technical short courses and workshops on ice cream technologies for ice cream manufacturers in November or December of every year. Course cost is about $1,500. Visit **www.onicecream.com** for more information.

2.5.3 Equipment Manufacturers Training Seminars

Many equipment manufacturers offer training seminars to industry professionals to teach them how to use their equipment. Once you have narrowed down your potential store niche, you can research equipment manufacturers for that product line. Check the manufacturers' websites to find out whether they offer any training.

Many ice cream equipment manufacturers also provide information on their websites about using their products. Some also offer ice cream, gelato, and sherbet or sorbet recipes that you can try out. See section 4.5.2 to find links to ice cream maker manufacturers' websites.

2.6 Resources for Self-Study

You can learn a lot about ice cream retail without formal education or taking a class. Many ice cream shops have websites, and exploring these sites will help you to learn more about them and the ice cream industry. You can also check out websites of trade associations (see section 2.4.2) and other online resources, all of which offer a variety of articles and resources. Following are some informal ways to learn more about the industry.

2.6.1 Industry Publications

An excellent way to learn about the ice cream retail industry is to read the trade publications read by people already in the industry. They will give you ideas for your own store, as well as tips on industry trends and practices.

- *The National Dipper*
  The National Dipper is a bi-monthly trade publication for owners of ice cream, frozen yogurt, and other frozen dessert retail stores. A few of the topics covered in recent issues include marketing ideas, promotions, and special events; industry outlook; menu development; equipment update; and choosing a mix supplier. The Classified ads in each issue post items for sale, including equipment and businesses. Current issues of The National Dipper are available by subscription only, but back issues are available for

$5.00 each (you can print off a form on their website to mail in your request). An annual source book with product, manufacturer, and distributor listings is also available for $35.
www.nationaldipper.com

- *Restaurants and Institutions*
Covering the entire foodservice industry, this publication claims—with good reason—that it is the industry's "most trusted source for food and business trend information and exclusive research." It offers a free subscription as well as online articles and reports. Enter "ice cream" in the search function to locate articles on topics of special interest to ice cream shop owners.
www.rimag.com

2.6.2 Books

Amazon.com lists more than 114,000 books on the subject of ice cream, but of course you do not have the time to read them all! So here is a selection of excellent books you may want to start with. Look for them at your local library, browse through them at a local bookstore, or order them online.

- *Ice Cream and Frozen Desserts: A Commercial Guide to Production and Marketing,*
by Malcolm Stogo

- *Ben & Jerry's, The Inside Scoop: How Two Real Guys Built a Business with Social Conscience and a Sense of Humor,*
by Fred Lager

- *The Ultimate Ice Cream Book: Over 500 Ice Creams, Sorbets, Granitas, Drinks, and More,*
by Bruce Weinstein

- *The Perfect Scoop: Ice Creams, Sorbets, Granitas, and Sweet Accompaniments,*
by David Lebovitz

- *Serendipity Sundaes: Ice Cream Constructions and Frozen Concoctions,*
by Stephen Bruce

- *A Passion for Ice Cream: 95 Recipes for Fabulous Desserts,* by Emily Luchetti and Sheri Giblin

- *The Science of Ice Cream,* by Chris Clarke

- *Ice Cream: The Delicious History,* by Marilyn Powell

2.6.3 Websites

Throughout this guide you will find numerous websites that can assist you in various aspects of starting and running an ice cream shop. In this section, we focus on several key resources that can help you quickly increase your knowledge. Each of these websites is a wealth of information that you can refer to throughout the process of starting your business.

Ice Cream and Frozen Desserts Recipe Sites

If you type "ice cream parlor" into a search engine, you will have over one million websites to choose from. Many of the general recipe websites such as Epicurious and Food Network have gourmet ice cream and other frozen dessert recipes you can try. There are also websites devoted to the ice cream industry (see section 2.4.2 for a list of association websites).

- *Epicurious*
  www.epicurious.com/tools/searchresults?search=gourmet+ice+cream&x=0&y=0

- *Food Network*
  www.foodnetwork.com/food/recipes/recipe/0,1977,FOOD_9936_144,00.html

- *World of Ice Cream*
  www.worldoficecream.com/Commercial_white_base.htm

- *Dairy Foods*
  www.dairyfoods.com

- *Ice-Cream-Recipes*
  www.ice-cream-recipes.com/making_ice_cream.htm

Other Online Resources

Online Forums

Another good source of acquiring information about ice cream trends, customer preferences, and different ice cream shops is through online message boards like Foodservice Forums. Following are a few of the sites that provide forums for people to post and read comments on ice cream or related topics.

- *Foodservice Forum*
  Foodservice provides multiple forums for topics related to the foodservice industry, such as customer loyalty, POS systems, and how to deal with customer complaints. Its forums are very active, with hundreds of threads and posted comments. A search box allows users to look for specific topics. A search for ice cream at the time of publication brought up over 500 threads that mentioned ice cream, with threads on ice cream scoopers, adding retail items, selling retail merchandise, a potential ice cream shop owner asking for advice, and shop owners' success with websites.
  http://forums.foodservice.com/?fid=0&token=0

- *Roadfood*
  Roadfood's Ice Cream & Custards forum includes comments posted by readers who want to know such things as whether a specific shop lives up to its reputation, what flavors are recommended at a certain shop, and what service is like at another. This message board is an excellent place to browse to learn what customers are looking for and what will turn them away from a shop and cause them to recommend that others avoid it.
  www.roadfood.com/Forums/forum.asp?FORUM_ID=17

- *Ice Cream New York*
  Ice Cream New York has an online forum similar to Roadfood. Free registration is required to view the ice cream forum.
  www.icecreamnewyork.com

Blogs

Blogs are another great source of information about ice cream trends, preferences, and shop practices. Written by both customers and shop owners, they offer a wealth of information on a vast array of topics. For example, A Daily Scoop provides reviews of ice cream, allowing ice cream lovers and shop owners to learn what flavors are hot – and which are not. Blogs allow shop owners the opportunity to discover what customers are seeking when they frequent an ice cream shop, what captures their attention, and what makes them look elsewhere. The following are a few blogs devoted to all things ice cream:

- *A Daily Scoop*
  http://adailyscoop.com

- *Ice Cream Journal*
  http://icecreamjournal.turkeyhill.com

- *The Ice Cream Diaries*
  ("One guy's account of the trials, tribulations, and offbeat characters from one old-fashioned ice cream and candy shop")
  http://icecreamdiaries.blogspot.com

- *A Blog of Ice Cream*
  www.ice-cream-recipes.com/blog/

- *All Things Ice Cream (Blog)*
  http://allthingsicecreamblog.com

- *A Vegan Ice Cream Paradise*
  http://veganicecream.blogspot.com

Online Videos

Online videos are a quick and easy way to survey a vast array of topics. Here are a few ideas for locating online videos on topics of interest to you.

Many franchises post videos on their website to give potential franchisees an overview of their stores and franchising opportunities. Watching a few of these videos can help viewers identify areas of concern and questions about their own potential store even if they are planning on owning an independent store or one in a different franchise. For those considering a specific franchise, the videos are an essential introduction to the company. See section 3.2.2 for a list of the top ice cream franchisors and their website addresses as well as for information on how to find websites of other franchise ice cream stores.

Culinary videos show hands-on demonstrations in a variety of subjects such as making homemade ice cream, baking waffle cones, and creating ice cream cakes. Visit All Recipes: How to Make Ice Cream (**http://allrecipes.com/HowTo/How-to-Make-Ice-Cream-Video/Detail.aspx**) to see an example of the kinds of video you can find online.

3. Starting Your Ice Cream Shop

Now that we've looked at ways to develop your business skills, it's time to look at how to go about actually starting your own store. This chapter of the guide will walk you step-by-step through the process.

Use the checklist below as a guideline to help you complete the steps necessary to get your business going. In fact, you may want to print the checklist and keep it nearby as you go through the rest of this guide so you can add items as you learn more about them.

Getting Started Basics Checklist

- Choose your niche.
- Prepare your business plan.
- Obtain a business license.
- Locate potential locations and weigh pros and cons of each.

- Secure financing.
- Lease or purchase store space.
- Obtain any necessary permits or certificates.
- Purchase store fixtures.
- Purchase software your store will use for inventory.
- Decide what merchandise you will offer for sale, locate suppliers and purchase inventory.
- Start advertising your grand opening.
- Decide if you need help. Interview and hire additional employees, if necessary.
- If you are planning to hire employees, obtain an Employee Identification Number (contact details later in this guide).
- Complete your store operations manual and finalize any store policies.
- Make a plan for your grand opening.
- Set up systems for record keeping.
- Set up window displays.
- Open your business.

3.1 Choosing Your Niche

The first thing to consider for your store is what types of products you will sell. This is your "niche" or specialty. You should try to remain flexible and not define your store's offerings too narrowly through your first year. This will help you to adapt to the needs of your clientele. You don't want to offer products that people aren't interested in buying.

Initially, as you consider what niche to fill with your own store, remember that the simplest approach is sell something you are familiar with. Look at areas of your life and experience to help you decide. Stick with what is familiar at first, and learn more as you go. Here are a few tips to help you choose your niche.

- Is there a need in your community for what you plan to sell? Can you effectively compete?

- Do some market research to give you an idea of trends in the industry you are entering. The best place to start is by studying other successful stores similar to the one you are planning to open. Don't be afraid to ask other retail store owners for their advice. You may hear that sales of certain types of products are booming, while some products may be losing popularity.

- Have any businesses similar to yours opened and closed in the area recently? If you're new to the area, you may have to speak to other business owners and locals to get this information. While your marketing and customer service might be better than the stores that closed, the fact that a similar store has been unsuccessful might indicate that a particular type of retail outlet doesn't do well in your area. If at all possible, try to track down the previous store owner through the local phone book and ask a few questions.

You'll find some additional resources for doing market research in section 3.4 on business planning to help you focus in on your market, but even if you already have an idea of your specialty, this section may help you refine it further. Below are a few ideas for specialized ice cream retail niches. In addition to these broad categories, ice cream shop owners have come up with many more specialty niches, such as party-only shops, shops with entertainment, and so on.

3.1.1 Old-Fashioned Ice Cream Parlor

Old fashioned ice cream parlors try to create an atmosphere that evokes nostalgia for days long past. Themes range from Victorian Age parlors to 1950s style soda shops, and everything in between. Typically, such a shop is found in a historically significant area of town or in a historical building location. They're often continuations of ice cream shop businesses that have been in business for decades.

Here are some of the common features of old-fashioned ice cream parlors:

- Home made ice cream made on site

- Unique "signature" flavors

- House specialty dishes like sundaes and banana splits
- Home made waffle cones
- Home made pastries, sandwiches, cookies, etc.
- Often coupled with an old-fashioned candy shop
- Wood or tile flooring
- Wooden booths for seating
- Tiffany-style lamps
- Pressed-tin ceilings
- Period fixtures and detailing (brass rails, antique furnishings, etc.)
- Old fashioned glassware, flatware
- Old fashioned signs and posters
- Historical memorabilia throughout the shop
- Showcase the works of local artists on their walls
- "Neighborhood" ice cream shop
- Roots and community ties (family business)
- Gimmicky touches like straw hats, candy-striped aprons, etc.

Here are some examples of old-fashioned ice cream parlors to give you some ideas for your own shop:

- *Jaxson's Ice Cream*
  www.jaxsonsicecream.com
- *Hoppie's*
  (Theme is mid-century soda fountain and ice cream parlor.)
  www.hoppies.com
- *The Franklin Fountain*
  www.franklinfountain.com/history.php

3.1.2 Scoop Shop

Scoop shops are the mainstay of the ice cream industry. They are smaller establishments, usually in the 400-600 square feet range. Most do not provide seating, since customers buy at a scoop display area and then leave with their purchases. Ben & Jerry's smaller scoop shops are typical examples.

Opening a scoop shop can be one of the least expensive ways to get into the ice cream business. Smaller size means smaller rent or build costs, for example. In addition, equipment and fixtures costs will be lower, since you won't need to outfit a smaller shop in the same way you would a larger shop with seating for customers.

The day-to-day operations costs are lower. Staffing levels are lower, you won't need a dishwasher or table servers, and you don't need to buy dishes and flatware. You probably won't be making your own ice cream but buying it from suppliers, keeping inventory costs lower.

Even smaller are kiosk-type scoop shops, which can be as small as 100 square feet. These are usually located in malls or other enclosed high foot-traffic public areas. Essentially, they are much like regular mall kiosks, but with ice cream storage and service areas in a complete enclosure. Breyer's Ice Cream offers a kiosk option (visit **www.breyerskiosk.com/breyerskiosk/solutions/**), as does Ben & Jerry's (**www.benjerry.com/scoop-shops/franchise-opportunities/start_up_costs.cfm**), although these can be expensive options.

Despite the small size, many scoop shops offer catering services such as birthday parties, scoop parties, ice cream socials, and so on. If offering catering services appeals to you, you can still offer these with a scoop shop establishment.

3.1.3 Ice Cream Trucks and Carts

Another alternative, especially if you are on a limited budget, is to purchase an ice cream truck or ice cream carts. This sub-sector of the industry is quite well represented and thousands of trucks and carts are on the road in North America. The association representing ice cream truck owners, the International Association of Ice Cream Vendors (see

www.iaicv.org), says that this niche is gaining in credibility as the quality of trucks and integrity of drivers increases.

Most ice cream trucks sell novelties and soft serve ice cream. Some trucks allow you to carry 80 or more gallons of soft serve mix that can make close to 3,000 4-ounce cones. Other trucks are designed to carry a certain quantity of novelties such as ice cream bars, milk shakes, popsicles, sundaes, and even nachos and hot dogs.

An ice cream truck comes with all the equipment you need on board and costs much less to purchase than an existing ice cream store or franchise. A truck to vend novelties will cost about $20,000, while a soft serve truck runs closer to $40,000; within the means of most people interested in getting into this sector of the business.

Also available in this part of the industry are ice cream carts for vending ice creams, gelatos, and novelties. These are the carts you see at festivals, and downtown sidewalks, or travelling through your neighborhood during the summer. Typical costs for these carts are $2,000 to $5,000.

To see a number of examples of ice cream truck and cart businesses, visit **www.cgl.uwaterloo.ca/~smann/IceCream/l-trucks.html**.

3.2 Options for Starting an Ice Cream Shop

Once you have decided on your niche, you'll need to decide whether to buy an existing store, buy a franchise, or open a new store. Deciding which route is right for you is an important decision.

An established store will cost more than starting from scratch, but it also comes with customers, inventory, and reputation, which means it's likely to continue with its pre-established success. A new store typically costs less to start up, and you can tailor it specifically to your own vision. Unlike buying an established store, though, you will need to spend more on advertising, gaining clientele, and making a reputation for your business — and new businesses have a higher risk of failure. Franchises might be another option to consider. We'll explain more about how these work in section 3.2.2.

3.2.1 Buying an Established Store

One way to start is to buy an existing business and make it your own. Buying an existing store can show you a profit on the very first day you're open. You'll still need a business plan, financing, a lawyer and an accountant, but many of the other decisions – like what to call it and where to locate it — will already be made. In addition, you will acquire all or most of the equipment, furniture, supplies, and inventory you will need to get started. You also get clientele and the established business name.

However, you should also look very careful at whatever else you might be acquiring. The business may have outstanding debts and you may have to assume any liabilities that come with the store, such as bills it owes to its suppliers, or repairs or maintenance expenditures that haven't been paid.

If this option for starting your business appeals to you, begin by looking for stores for sale in your area. Do not be afraid to approach local store owners and inquire if they are interested in selling their business, or if they know any store owners considering retirement. And, don't forget to look in your local newspaper, local business publications, and contact the Chamber of Commerce for information on shops that may possibly be for sale.

What to Look for Before You Buy

Purchasing an existing business can be a good way to get into the retail trade immediately, but there are a few cautions. You could be purchasing a failed business with a poor financial history, bad reputation, or even some hidden liabilities as mentioned earlier. You need to perform a due diligence investigation, meaning you need to look at the operations of the business, including revenues, cash flow, assets and liabilities, licensing, and so on, before purchasing.

To protect yourself, before making a deal for any business hire an accountant to go over the company's books. This will help you to determine if the seller is representing the business accurately and honestly. Then, before signing an Agreement of Purchase and Sale, you should enlist the services of a lawyer to review the written agreement.

Following are a few things to look for as you start your search for an existing business to buy.

Why is the business for sale?

Here are a few of the most common reason why business owners offer their businesses for sale:

- The owner is retiring or has health problems
- The owner is moving on to another store or another business altogether
- The business has failed and the owner wants to get out as quickly as possible
- The owner is afraid of increasing competition
- One key element of their business strategy is faulty, such as the type of inventory offered
- The business is part of a chain and is not doing as well as other stores owned by the same company
- A partnership has fallen apart and the partners are liquidating all or a part of the company's assets

Before purchasing an existing retail business answer the following important questions (with assistance from the seller whenever possible).

- Why is the vendor selling the business?
- What is the sales history of the store?
- What is the average cost to maintain the store?
- What assets or liabilities will come with the purchase?
- Are there any tax, legal or property issues you will have to contend with?

The previous owner may help you with many of these issues or you may have to do your own research, perhaps by consulting local government, realtors or other merchants. Whatever the situation, you should never buy an existing business without knowing all of the details.

You should have complete access to the previous owner's store records, including financial statements. With these you will have information about the customer base and noticeable patterns in the store's business practices. Unwillingness by the previous owner to provide financial statements for your complete inspection might be a tip-off that something isn't right with the business.

Potential buyers often work in the store for a short time before purchasing it. Owners are often willing to train the buyer. If the business owner you are thinking about buying from is unwilling to do this, you should find out why.

Hidden Costs

When you purchase an established business it seems like you're purchasing a turnkey operation with license, location, traffic and inventory all in place and you just have to open the doors. However, there may be hidden expenses that you will have to pay for, such as back taxes, needed repairs or building code violations, so be sure to watch for these. You don't want an angry supplier showing up at your door demanding money for inventory purchased by the previous owner but never paid for. (You've already purchased the inventory from the owner and now you'll have to pay for it a second time.)

In addition to paying for the business, and any miscellaneous expenses, you will also need money to pay for equipment and supplies, and additional inventory. You may also want to start a marketing campaign in order to make people aware of the fact that you're the new owner and let the community know that you're open for business. This is particularly important if you've bought a business that might have been on the decline for whatever reasons.

Finally, if you plan to remodel a store after buying it, perhaps to give it a fresh new image, then that could easily become another significant expense depending on the size of the job and the contractor you hire. Keep all these additional potential costs in mind as you consider buying the existing business.

Creating a Spec Sheet

A spec sheet is a summary of the business and includes the book value (total assets minus total liabilities and goodwill), market value (the book value figure adjusted to reflect the current market value of assets), and the liquidation value (how much the owner could raise if the business was liquidated). Earnings potential should also be considered.

If the value you arrive at is significantly different from what the owner is asking for the business, ask the seller how he or she arrived at the price. You can then make your offer based on your estimate of worth and the owner's asking price. You don't need to accept that the business is actually worth what the owner thinks it is.

The real worth of a business is in its continuing profitability, so examine the financial records closely (especially the profit and loss statements and cash flow statements) to get a good idea of what your revenue would be, as well as your expenses and net income. Try to buy a business for its annual profit. Don't be distracted by the listed price.

One helpful resource is the Due Diligence Checklist at FindLaw.com. The full website address is **http://smallbusiness.findlaw.com/starting-business** (click on "More Topics", then on "Buying an Existing Business" then on "Due Diligence Checklist" under Tools & Resources). This checklist shows you everything that you should check out about any business you're thinking of purchasing in areas like the business's organization and good standing, financial statements, physical assets, real estate, and much more. Be sure to consult this checklist or one like it as you perform your due diligence investigation.

The Canada Business Services for Entrepreneurs website has an excellent page at **www.canadabusiness.ca/eng/125/140** (scroll down to "Determining how much to pay for the business"), that details everything you need to consider when purchasing an existing business. Information includes advice on how to determine asset and earnings value, how to valuate a business and a detailed list of questions to ask when looking at a business you're thinking of purchasing.

What will an existing retail store cost?

Purchase prices are determined by a number of factors. These include region and neighborhood location, profit and local economy, potential growth, and the owner's own sense of what the company is worth based on reputation or goodwill. BusinessesforSale.com, Business Nation, the Business Resale Network and others offer listings of many types of businesses that, for whatever reason, are being offered for sale. These sites list each business's asking price, and usually state its turnover and profit.

Expect to pay anywhere from $60,000 to upwards of $300,000 for an existing independently owned ice cream shop. Franchised ice cream shops can cost anywhere from $75,000 to $900,000. This usually will include all contents of the shop and often means taking over an existing lease or rental agreement for the location. Starting your own store requires a lot of energy and devotion — whether you build from scratch or buy an existing store. You should plan on waiting two to five years to earn back your purchase price.

Recent listings of ice cream businesses for sale (all on leased premises) on these websites included an ice cream shop selling scooped ice cream, yogurt, and smoothies in Southern California asking $79,000, complete with all of the shop's equipment and furnishings. An ice creamery and sweets cafe in New Jersey for $86,000, with all equipment included. A popular 20-seat ice cream shop at the higher end of the scale in a tourist area in the Midwest asking $350,000 for the business, with all equipment included.

- *BusinessesforSale.com*
  (Includes business for sale in the U.S., Canada, U.K. and other countries)
  www.businessesforsale.com

- *Business Nation*
  www.businessnation.com/Businesses_for_Sale/

- *BizQuest*
  www.bizquest.com/buy

- *BizBen*
  (California only)
  www.bizben.com

Try entering the keywords "ice cream parlor" or "ice cream shop" into each website's search engine or search by industry.

TIP: Beware of websites that require a fee or ask for personal information to view their listings. Real Estate agents make their money on sales and not on people browsing.

Financing

Some owners will allow you to finance an existing business if you can come up with a good down payment but are unable to purchase it outright. Many of the owners of the businesses for sale at the websites above are willing to negotiate financing with potential buyers. Be sure you understand the terms of any financing you set up with the seller. See a lawyer before agreeing to anything.

If you are considering borrowing from a lending institution such as a bank then financing an existing, profitable business is much less of a risk than starting a new one. A lending institution will want to see your detailed business plan before agreeing to lend you any money. (See section 3.4 for more on how to write a business plan, and section 3.5 for more about financing your new business venture.)

Making an Offer

When you have done your research, figured out what the business is worth and decided you want to buy the business you may then decide to make an offer, possibly less than the asking price based on your own valuation of the business. Usually the owner then will make a counter-offer. Keep in mind that you may have less leeway to negotiate a better purchase price if the owner will be financing the purchase for you.

You will usually be asked to pay a non-refundable deposit. This is standard and ensures the owner that you are a serious buyer. Be sure to get a deposit receipt and get any purchase agreement in writing after you've arrived at a mutually agreeable price. Also be sure that every important detail about the purchase is mentioned in the contract. Because so much money is at risk, a lawyer should draw up or at least review the contract before either party signs.

Buying an Existing Building

A second option rather than buying an entire business is to buy an existing building in which to set up shop and then move your business into it. The obvious advantage here is that buying an existing building often is less expensive than buying an established business along with the building housing it. Another aspect to consider is that, as already mentioned, if you buy an existing business you inherit both advantages and disadvantages from the previous owner.

One advantage of buying a building is that it most likely has already passed fire and building codes, unlike a new project that will require inspections and approval by municipal authorities before you can occupy it. Be sure to check first with zoning laws to be sure you're safe to operate your business there.

There are disadvantages as well. The building may require heavy infrastructure repairs (such as utilities or plumbing) or you might have to completely remodel the interior. Repair and remodeling costs can be expensive, even into thousands of dollars, so be sure to inspect the building carefully for any structural problems before you buy it.

Do a thorough investigation of the building's interior and exterior. Check the electrical systems, cooling and ventilation systems, bathrooms, walls and ceilings. If possible, interview the previous owner and ask about any potential problems that might create extra costs for you.

You should consider hiring a building inspector to conduct a thorough, professional evaluation of the property. Hiring a professional building inspector, though an added cost to buying a building, could save you from a disastrous purchase (and thousands of dollars in repairs) so consider finding one to look at any property you're thinking about purchasing. To find building inspectors in your area, check the Yellow Pages under "Building Inspection Service."

3.2.2 Franchising

If you are eager to start your own store, but are concerned about the many facets involved in getting everything set up, you may want to consider franchising.

Franchising is a business model which allows someone (you) to run a local business using an established regional or national company or corporation name, logo, products, services, marketing and business systems. The original company is known as the "franchisor" and the company that is granted the right to run its business the same way as the franchisor is known as the "franchisee."

You have probably bought products and services from many franchises. Burger King, Wendy's and many other fast-food outlets are franchises, as are many others. Recent figures from industry analysts estimate that franchising companies and their franchisees accounted for more than $1 trillion in annual U.S. retail sales from 760,000 franchised small businesses in 75 industries so clearly franchises can be very successful business models to start with.

Pros and Cons of Franchising

> *"Buying a franchise allows an individual to start a business with considerable help and assistance from the franchisor. For an individual to open a business on his/her own is a scary prospect, and if he/she does not have much business experience, he/she could come up against some unexpected obstacles. Buying a franchise enables the individuals to work with the franchisor and to learn from their prior experiences and mistakes, in order to enhance the likelihood of their own success."*
>
> — Aaron Serruya, cofounder, Yogen Fruz,
> Toronto, Ontario, Canada

Often, people who choose to franchise do so because they want to minimize their risk. By working with an established system, franchisees hope to avoid costly mistakes and make a profit more quickly, especially since the business probably already has name recognition, products and marketing concepts that are popular among the public.

Franchising offers some unique advantages. Buying a ready-made business means you do not have to agonize over the minute details of a business plan, you do not have to create a logo and letterhead, and the organization of your store is already done. Plus, there is less risk with a ready-made business with a proven track record.

Franchises are good for people who want support running their businesses. The franchisee may receive assistance with everything from obtaining supplies to setting up record keeping systems. Many franchisors are continuously working to develop better systems and products and you can take advantage of those developments.

Franchisors typically provide a complete business plan for managing and operating the establishment. The plan provides step-by-step procedures for major aspects of the business and provides a complete matrix for the management decisions confronted by its franchisees.

If you choose to franchise, remember that although you own the store you do not own any of the trademarks or business systems. A franchisee must run their business according to the terms of their agreement with the franchisor. In exchange for the security, training, and marketing power of the franchise trademark, you must be willing to give up some of your independence. If you are a person who likes to make most decisions on your own or to chart the course of your business alone, a franchise may not be right for you.

Since someone else is ultimately "in charge," you may be wondering how having a franchise is different than being an employee. In fact, there are significant differences. You have more freedom than an employee; for example, you might choose your own working hours. And you could ultimately earn a lot more money than an employee.

On the other hand, franchisees must pay thousands of dollars up front for the opportunity to work with the business. In addition, you will be required to cover your own operating costs (including the cost of staffing your store to the levels required by the franchisor), pay a franchise fee and a percentage of total sales.

Costs

Entrepreneur Magazine describes a franchise fee as a one-time charge paid to the franchisor "for the privilege of using the business concept, attending their training program, and learning the entire business." Other start-up costs may include the products and services you will actually need to run the business, such as supplies, store fixtures, computer equipment, advertising, etc.

The fees for operation will vary from franchise to franchise, and may rely heavily on location, but expect the franchise fee to be somewhere between $12,500 - $42,000, with additional start-up costs.

There are a variety of factors involved in determining the initial investment. For example, if you are interested in operating a Marble Slab Creamery franchise in the United States, the average investment will cost anywhere between $225,275 - $376,375 depending on the geographic location and the size of the store. In Canada, the average investment for this franchise would be $293,300. In general, these investment figures are higher in Canada.

Most franchise owners obtain financing for their business by providing approximately 35% of the total capital, and then arrange a business loan from a local bank for the balance of the total investment required. (See section 3.5 for more information on start-up financing.)

In addition to your initial investment, you can expect to pay the franchisor ongoing royalties, generally on a monthly basis. These royalties are usually calculated as a percentage of your gross monthly sales, and typically range from 3 percent to as much as 12 percent; the exact amount will depend on the company you franchise with. This is the corporation's cut for providing you with their business model and good name.

Choosing an Ice Cream Shop Franchise

It is important to do your homework on the company you are interested in franchising with — gather all the information you need to make an informed decision. Speak with other people who have invested in the company you are investigating and have an attorney examine the franchisor's contract.

Get some professional opinions on any franchise opportunity you're interested in. Work with an attorney who understands the laws associated with franchising. Also, you may want to work with an accountant to examine your anticipated expenses, your financing needs, and your prospects for achieving your desired level of profitability before you sign any agreement.

Key points to research:

- The type of experience required in the franchised business
- Hours and personal commitment necessary to run the business

- Background of the franchisor or corporation
- Success rate of other franchisees in the same system
- Franchising fees to open the franchise
- Initial total investment required to open the franchise
- Cost of operation to continue the right to operate the business as a franchisee
- Any additional fees, products or services, such as advertising, that you must buy from the franchisor and how they are supplied

For excellent advice on franchising, visit the following websites:

- *Canadian Franchise Association*
  www.cfa.ca
- *Entrepreneur's Franchise Zone*
  www.entrepreneur.com/franchises/index.html
- *Small Business Administration: Buying a Franchise*
  www.sba.gov/smallbusinessplanner/start/buyafranchise/index.html

Websites that provide comprehensive lists and links to franchises for the ice cream industry include the following:

- *Franchising.com*
  www.franchising.com/opportunities/food/dessert/
- *Franchise Gator*
  www.franchisegator.com/Ice-Cream-Franchises/
- *Franchise Opportunities*
  www.franchiseopportunities.com/industries/30/Ice_Cream_Yogurt_Fro.htm
- *Red Hot Franchises*
  www.redhotfranchises.com/franchises/Food_and_Restaurants/Ice_Cream_Shops

There are a large number of companies offering franchise opportunities in the ice cream shop market. Their specialties are varied so no matter what type of retail franchise you're interested in, you'll probably find one that fits your needs and interests. Here are a few well known franchises for you to consider.

> **NOTE:** The following list does not represent an endorsement by FabJob or the author, of any of these businesses. They are provided for information purposes only. Only you know which franchise, if any, is right for you.

American Dairy Queen Corporation

Dairy Queen has two types of franchise stores: The DQ Grill & Chill is the flagship concept featuring Dairy Queen ice cream products and a food menu. The Treat Center combines the Dairy Queen products with Orange Julius fruit smoothies and beverages.

Dairy Queen offers multiple franchise options, including the standard program for individuals who want to own one store and programs aimed at individuals who want to own multiple units or invest in a Dairy Queen franchise without operating it. Dairy Queen offers franchisees assistance in site selection and new store project coordination and also provides three to five weeks of training, field support, and marketing support, including regional and national campaigns.

Contact Info

Address:	7505 Metro Boulevard Minneapolis, MN 55439
Phone:	(952) 830-0200
Contact:	**www.dairyqueen.com/us-en/own-a-dq/request-info/**
Website:	**www.dairyqueen.com**
Franchise Fee:	DQ Grill & Chill: $35,000, 4% royalty on sales, and 5-6% ongoing sales promotion fees gross Treat Center: $25,000, 6% royalty on sales, and 3-6% ongoing sales promotion fees gross

Initial Investment:	For a standard, free standing DQ Grill & Chill (excluding land): $995,000-$1,610,000 (not including franchise fees) For a standard mall-location Treat Center: $345,000-$375,000 (not including franchise fees)

Baskin-Robbins

Baskin-Robbins has over 5,800 stores in 34 countries serving soft serve and scoop ice cream—with over 2,700 stores in the United States and over 100 in Canada. Owned by Dunkin' Brands Inc., Baskin-Robbins offers franchisees assistance in site selection, design and construction support, training programs, marketing support, and technology support.

Contact Info

Address:	600 N Brand Boulevard, Suite 600 Glendale, CA 91203
Phone:	(818) 241-2485; (800) 859-5339
Contact:	**franchiseinfo@baskinrobbins.com** (email) or 800-777-9983 (phone)
Website:	**www.baskinrobbins.com**
Franchise Fee:	$20,000 - $30,000; 5.9% royalty fee
Initial Investment:	$156,900 - $560,400 (including franchise fee)

Ben & Jerry's

Almost everyone who has heard of ice cream has heard of Ben & Jerry's. It is a company known for its commitment to social activism as well as its superior ice cream. In 2000, Unilever purchased the company. Today there are over 430 scoop shops in the United States and 21 shops in Canada. Ben & Jerry's offers several types of shops, including a kiosk scoop shop. Ben & Jerry's offers franchisees assistance with site selection and initial and ongoing training and support.

Contact Info

Address: 30 Community Drive
South Burlington, VT 05403

Phone: (802) 846-1500

Contact: (802) 846-1543, EXT. 7831

Website: **www.benjerry.com**

Franchise Fee: $32,000; 3% royalty, and 4% marketing contribution

Initial Investment: $118,300 - $385,000 (including franchise fee)

Bruster's Real Ice Cream

Bruster's has more than 250 ice cream parlors in the eastern United States. Bruster's product line includes ice cream, sherbet, yogurt, and cakes. Bruster's offers franchisees the option to own or lease a store. Potential franchisees can learn more about Bruster's by participating in one of its Taste of Bruster's Seminars, which provide a store tour as well as in-depth information about owning a Bruster's franchise. Bruster's Real Ice Cream offers franchisees assistance in site selection; classroom and on-site training; and ongoing support from project management, operations, and financing and marketing professionals.

Contact Info

Address: 730 Mulberry Street
Bridgewater, PA 15009

Phone: 724-774-4250

Contact: **www.brustersicecream.com/own_a_brusters/inforequest.asp** (online contact form)

Lori Molnar, (724) 774-4250 ext. 109 (phone)

Website: **www.brustersicecream.com**

Franchise Fee: $35,000; 5% royalty fee

Initial Investment: $172,000 - $1,200,000 (including franchise fee). Average base cost of entry is $350,000 excluding land and development costs

Carvel Corporation

Carvel sells soft serve ice cream, hand-dipped ice cream products, and character-shaped ice cream cakes at about 500 franchised outlets in the United States. The majority of the outlets are found in high-traffic areas such as malls, airports, and sports stadiums. Founded by Tom Carvel, a traveling salesman, in 1934, the chain is now owned by FOCUS Brands.

Contact Info

Address:	200 Glenridge Point Parkway, Suite200 Atlanta, GA 30342
Phone:	(404) 255-3250; (800) 227-8353
Contact:	800-227-8353 (Franchising Inquiry Phone Line)
	www.carvel.com/franchise_opportunity/index.html (Request Info form)
Website:	**www.carvel.com**
Franchise Fee:	$30,000
Initial Investment:	$46,000 - $388,700 (including franchise fee)

Cold Stone Creamery

Kahala Corporation's Cold Stone Creamery has more than 1,400 premium ice cream outlets in the world, including over 1,300 in the United States. Cold Stone Creamery offers franchisees assistance in site location and analysis; lease negotiations and review; and construction coordination during build-out process. It provides two weeks of intensive training; logistics and store opening support; national marketing and public relations campaigns, and other marketing support.

Contact Info

Address:	9311 E. Via de Ventura Scottsdale, AZ 85258
Phone:	(480) 362-4800; (866) 464-9467

Contact:	For contact information for the Area Developer in your area, go to **https://www.coldstonecreamery.com/franchises/areadeveloper.asp** or email **info@coldstonecreamery.com**
Website:	**www.coldstonecreamery.com**
Franchise Fee:	$42,000; 6% royalty fees
Initial Investment:	$294,000-$439,000 (including the franchise fee)

Dippin' Dots, Inc.

Over 400 franchised vendors in the United States sell Dippin' Dots' ice cream, yogurt, flavored ice, and ice cream cakes. Its name derives from the tiny beads of flash-frozen ice cream, yogurt, sherbert, and flavored ice used in its products. Outlets include both kiosks and stores in malls, amusement parks, movie theaters, schools, and sports arena. Dippin' Dots offers franchisees assistance with site selection and ordering and inventory control processes.

Contact Info

Address:	1640 McCracken Boulevard, Suite 100 Paducah, KY 42001
Phone:	(270) 575-6990
Contact:	**www.dippindots.com/contact/** (Contact Form)
Website:	**www.dippindots.com**
Franchise Fee:	$12,500; 4% royalty fee
Initial Investment:	$80,420 - $235,250

Friendly's Ice Cream Corporation

Friendly's operates a chain of over 500 family-style restaurants that specialize in ice cream and dessert treats, 198 of which are franchised stores. Friendly's offers franchisees assistance in real estate selection and site evaluation, construction planning and development, and product research and menu development. It provides ongoing operational, marketing, and public relations support, staff training resources, product purchasing programs, and a cost efficient distribution system.

Contact Info

Address:	1855 Boston Rd. Wilbraham, MA 01095
Phone:	(413) 731-4000; (800) 966-9970
Contact:	(800) 966-9970 or **franchising@friendlys.com**
Website:	**www.friendlys.com**
Franchise Fee:	$35,000; 4% royalty on sales, and marketing fee of 3.5% of gross sales
Initial Investment:	$462,300 - $2,100,000

Haagen-Dazs Company Inc.

Haagen-Dazs ice cream parlors are operated by Dreyer's, a subsidiary of Nestle. Haagen-Dazs franchise stores include both stores and kiosks in malls. Haagen-Dazs offers franchisees assistance in site location analysis; construction and development. It provides two-week training at company headquarters; on-site store training and assistance; and ongoing marketing, promotional, operational, and business support.

Contact Info

Address:	5929 College Ave. Oakland, CA 94618
Phone:	(763) 293-2691; (800) 767-0120
Contact:	**www.haagendazs.com/company/franchise/franchise_consideration.aspx** (Request Form)
Website:	**www.haagendazs.com**
Franchise Fee:	$30,000
Initial Investment:	$80,000 - $200,000

MaggieMoo's International, LLC

MaggieMoo's International operates close to 200 MaggieMoo's Ice Cream & Treatery shops in the United States and Thailand. The shops sell super-premium ice cream that is mixed with the customer's selection of candy, fruit, and nuts, and are located in malls, lifestyle centers, airports, outlets, and city storefronts. MaggieMoo's offers franchisees assistance in site selection and store leasing, construction, purchasing, training, store operations, quality control, advertising and promotions, research and development, and marketing.

Contact Info

Address:	10025 Governor Warfield Pkwy., Ste. 301 Columbia, MD 21044
Phone:	(410) 740-2100; (800) 949-8114
Contact:	**info@maggiemoos.com**
Website:	**www.maggiemoos.com**
Franchise Fee:	$33,000; 6% royalty; 2% marketing contribution
Initial Investment:	$225,000 - $375,000 (includes franchise fee)

Marble Slab Creamery, Inc.

Marble Slab Creamery has over 550 stores in the United States, Canada, Puerto Rico, and the United Arab Emirates. The company offers franchisees assistance with site selection, lease negotiations, architectural layout and construction, and store opening. It provides ten days of training, continued field supervision, public relations assistance, and an advertising program.

Contact Info

Address:	1346 Oakbrook Dr., Suite 170 Norcross, GA 30093
Phone:	(770) 514-4500
Contact:	**info@marbleslab.com**
Website:	**www.marbleslab.com**
Franchise Fee:	U.S: $22,000 - $32,000; 6% royalty on gross sales; advertising fee of 2% of gross sales Canada: $25,000; 6% royalty; 2 % advertising fee
Initial Investment:	$225,000 - $375,000 (includes franchise fee) Canada: $293,300 (includes franchise fee)

Yogen Fruz Worldwide

Yogen Fruz is a frozen yogurt franchise that started in Canada with one shop and now has over 1,100 franchisees in 20 countries worldwide. They offer training at the franchisee's location and at company headquarters. Yogen Fruz runs national and regional advertising campaigns on a co-op basis. Each new location is expected to hold a grand opening. On-going support includes Internet exposure, regular company meetings, and instruction and training in security and safety procedures.

Contact Info

Address:	210 Shields Court Markham, Ontario L3R 8V2
Phone:	(905) 479-8762
Contact:	**www.yogenfruz.com/home/en/franchise**
Franchise Fee:	$25,000; 6% royalty fee; renewal fee of 50% current franchise fee.
Initial Investment:	$150,000-$200,000

3.2.3 Opening a New Ice Cream Shop

Of course, you can always start from scratch and open a brand new store. That way, you can have complete control over every step of the process and make sure that your shop is everything you want it to be. The information in the rest of this chapter will show you how to do that.

3.3 Choosing a Store Name

If you decide to start up your own store from square one, choosing a name may be one of the most important decisions you make for your new business. You want something catchy that will draw people into the store while clearly indicating it is an ice cream shop.

If you have the financial resources, you could hire a naming professional to help you choose the right name for your company. Known as name consultants or naming firms, these organizations are experts at creating names, and can help you with trademark laws.

TIP: Business names don't have to be trademarked, but having them trademarked prevents anyone else from using the same name. Trademark laws are complicated, so if you think you want your company name trademarked it's a good idea to consult a lawyer with expertise in that area.

Most people starting up a new retail store, however, don't have the money necessary to hire professional name consultants. The cost of these services can start at a few thousand dollars. Instead, to come up with a name yourself, consider your niche and what types of customers you are trying to reach. You might even hold a brainstorming session and enlist family and friends for suggestions. If somebody comes up with a really good name, you'll probably know it right away.

Many ice cream shops are named after a person (usually the owner or owners), location, geographical feature, or landmark. Some shop owners hold contests in the community to name their new store, generating interest in the shop and community goodwill before it opens. Keep in mind that the name should be easy to say and remember.

Here are a few name samples from the store owners we surveyed.

- The Bent Spoon
- Capannari Ice Cream
- Carvel
- Marble Slab Creamery
- Rita's Water Ice
- Yogen Fruz

In most jurisdictions, once you have chosen your business name you will also have to file a "Doing Business As" (DBA) application, to register the fictitious name under which you will conduct your business operations. The DBA allows you to operate under a name other than your own legal name.

Filing a DBA usually takes place at the county level, although some states require that you file at the state level, publish your intent to operate under an assumed business name, and sign an affidavit stating that you have done so. However, in most cases it's usually just a short form to fill out and a small filing fee that you pay to your state or provincial government.

You can find links at the Business.gov website to the appropriate government departments where you can file your business name at **www.business.gov/register/business-name/dba.html**.

Trademarked Business Names

A trademark database lists all registered and trademarked business names. In the U.S., the essential place to start is with the U.S. Patent and Trademark Office. You can hire a company that specializes in this type of service to do a name search for you, if you choose. However, you can do an online search of the federal trademark database yourself to determine whether a name has already been registered.

You can also do this at the county level or at the state level when you file for a DBA using the fictitious names database of the agency you're filing with. The fictitious names database is where non-trademarked business names are listed.

You can check trademarks at the United States Patent and Trademark Office (**www.uspto.gov/main/trademarks.htm**). In Canada, the default database for name searches is the Newly Upgraded Automated Name Search (NUANS). You can search the NUANS database at **www.nuans.com**. There is a $20 charge for each NUANS search.

If you would like to learn more about this subject, you can read an in-depth article about naming your business entitled "How to Name Your Business" at the Entrepreneur.com website. This article includes tips on how to brainstorm ideas for naming your business, as well as establishing trademarks and how to file a DBA. A related article, "8 Mistakes to Avoid When Naming Your Business" offers tips on avoiding some typical business naming mistakes. You can find both of these articles at **www.entrepreneur.com/startingabusiness/startupbasics/index144024.html** (click on "Naming Your Business" in the "Browse by Topic" section).

3.4 Your Business Plan

> *"Make sure your business plan is conservative and reachable. Do not expect to make money in the first twelve months in most cases."*
>
> — Gary Bales, president, Carvel Corporation, Atlanta, Georgia

Many business owners fail not because their business ideas weren't great but rather because of their lack of planning. A business plan is a detailed breakdown of every aspect of your business, including its location, sources of start-up funding, aspects of financial planning and an in-depth description of your proposed business. A good business plan serves two purposes. It's your guide (one that can be used and modified as necessary on an ongoing basis) for how you want your company to progress and grow.

Your business plan also serves as a sales tool should you decide to seek outside funding for your business. A business plan is essential in meeting with your bank manager or other lending institution. They need to know you are a good risk before they loan you money. A business plan tells them that you are prepared and know where you're going.

Additionally, a well-thought out plan will help you to identify any factors that will affect your profits and your competitive advantages. A business plan will allow you to step back from your excitement about starting a business, and take an objective look at your plans.

A good plan will help you over the rough spots by identifying where you might have slow cash flow during certain seasons (e.g., during the summer when many people are away vacationing). A well-prepared plan will help you learn who your customers and competition are, to understand the strengths and weaknesses of your business, and to recognize factors that could affect the growth of your company.

You shouldn't treat your business plan as if its contents are written in stone, however. There are many reasons why you'll want to keep up-to-date with your business plan. As your business changes and grows, your business plan probably will need some tweaking to reflect new goals and changing customer purchasing patterns, for example. (You might find that certain products sell better than others as you move forward.) Your business plan description will need to change if you branch out into a different product niche in your store.

In the next section, we'll guide you through the various elements of your business plan and how they fit into the overall conception of your new enterprise.

3.4.1 What to Include in a Business Plan

A business plan can be a simple description of your business concept or a detailed report, including graphs and charts of potential growth. A typical business plan should include the following items. You will learn more about a number of the important items, such as marketing and store operations, later in this guide.

Cover Page

The cover page should list your name, home address, phone number and any other contact information you wish to provide. This is an often-overlooked, yet essential, piece of the business plan. If you are presenting your plan to investors or the bank, they must know how to contact you.

Executive Summary

This should be an upbeat explanation of your overall concept. Think of the paragraphs on the backs of book covers. An executive summary encapsulates the major contents of your business plan just as the paragraphs summarize the plot of a book. You want to sell your idea, so you need to keep it positive.

You should write the Executive Summary after the rest of the sections are completed (except, of course, the Table of Contents). The Executive Summary is the synopsis of your business vision. It should be concise and explain the major contents of your business plan. Be sure to include the following important points:

- Business start date and location
- Financial objectives for the year

- Commitment to resources (inventory, facilities, staff)
- Products and services
- A strong closing statement

Table of Contents

Make it easy for your investors by including a Table of Contents so they can easily turn to specific items such as your profit projections.

A Table of Contents, although it's the first thing to appear in the plan, should be the last thing you write. That way you already have all the content and page numbers in place.

Description

The description of your business should cover the products and services you plan to offer and be as specific as possible. You can also include industry information about other retail stores in your niche market. In this section of your business plan, you will include the following:

- *Products and Services:* What type of merchandise and services you will be offering to customers and any additional product lines or services you hope to add.
- *Customers:* This is the section to give an overview of who you think your typical customers will be.
- *Goals:* What would you like to achieve by opening your store? To establish yourself as a specialist in a certain sector of the industry? Expand your store to a larger operation in five years? Describe your business goals in this section.
- *Store Appearance:* Describe how your store will look from the front window display, the flooring, to the sign outside. Include merchandise display features, how traffic will flow through the store, as well as the total square footage of your retail space.
- *Unique Features:* What will separate your shop from others? What strengths will your business have over other similar businesses in your community? What previously unfilled product or service

area of the industry are you filling? This will also be a part of your marketing section.

- *Management:* In this section describe the store's ownership and explain its legal structure, whether or not you intend to hire employees, and what training you will offer to them.
- *Start-Up Costs:* Lenders are particularly interested in how much you need to get your business running. Provide an overview of your financing requirements, including your own investment contribution, and any additional sources of working capital; explain your business registration, licenses, and insurance. This will be only a summary description. More in-depth descriptions and details about finances will follow in your financial section.

While you should include some details about all of the items above, remember that the business description section provides only an overview. This is to give readers of your business plan a quick summary of how the store will be set up, your starting financial position, and an overview of the management and operation of your store. Some parts will obviously overlap with the more detailed information provided in the other sections.

Legal Structure

The next section to include is how your store will be set up from a legal standpoint. Here you will describe the legal structure of your business, such as sole proprietorship, partnership or corporation. This section may be included with the description of your business, or you can include it under a separate heading. Like other parts of your business plan, you can rearrange the sections or group them together. (You'll learn more about business legal structures in section 3.6.1 a little later in this chapter.)

Location

If you have not already chosen a location, then explain the type of space you wish to lease or purchase, and why you think it is a prime location for your store. If you need help finding a location, contact a local realtor to find out what is available for lease. If you have already chosen a location, then describe it and detail the positive points about where it is situated and why the site will be a good one for your business.

Your Market

Who are your potential customers and why? Use census information (see box below) to show you have done your homework. Include any information on upcoming construction or stores that may be planning to build in the neighborhood. You can get this information from your local zoning board, as new businesses will have to obtain permits from them.

How to Find Information on Your Market

Before opening your store in a particular area, find out if the market is right. For example, if the business you want to open requires a certain demographic (particular population characteristics) and that demographic is under-represented or lacking entirely, or if there are already several store similar to your own in the neighborhood, then you will need to decide if it's worthwhile starting your business in that area.

It is important to research this topic thoroughly. It could be vital to the success of your business. Census reports will help you with general information such as the average age of a city's residents or the number of children in the area. You can locate your area's latest census data at the U.S. Census Bureau website (**www.census.gov**) or Statistics Canada's census pages at **www12.statcan.ca/English/census**.

A visit to your local realty office can also prove worthwhile. Many realty companies keep statistics on the types of families moving into the area. It is also a good idea to talk to your local government (the zoning board is a good place to start) and find out if any permits have been granted for housing or business development. New housing additions often attract young families, whereas condominiums and apartments may be more likely to attract singles to the area.

Another good place to look is on the website of your local municipality. These websites often have employment statistics about local industries, level of education of the populace, and other important economic data. The local Chamber of Commerce can also provide similar information. Another website you can check out is **www.city-data.com**, where you can click on your state then your locality to find basic population and other related data.

For example, let's say that a complementary business or other facility, one that might bring additional customers into your store, is scheduled to open the week before your store opens. A new daycare facility opening nearby might bring in extra customers for a store offering children's products, or a new movie theatre in the neighborhood might attract an evening clientele for a restaurant; these are examples of complementary businesses. The opening of such a complementary business could potentially bring you a lot of extra customers, just as a new school, new housing development, and many other establishments could provide new customers.

Competition

List your competition. While it may not be a good idea to list every single competitor, it is a good idea to list a couple of the toughest ones. This will show the bank or investors you have realistic expectations about your business and are aware of what you need to do to survive. You can find where these stores are located by asking area residents or checking your local Yellow Pages.

Marketing

How will you determine your target market and then get the word out about your new business? Be detailed here. List specific marketing campaigns you plan to use; for example, local newspaper ads, flyers, and special signs. (To learn more about marketing see Chapter 6.)

Inventory and Pricing

Here, you will explain how you plan to acquire goods. List any suppliers you plan to work with, and what items you will need for the daily operation of your store. You may have to estimate prices, so your homework on other stores and what they offer and the prices they charge will be invaluable.

A good rule of thumb for estimating what you should sell an item for is to price it at double the price of your cost for the item. For example, if you have a product that you purchased for $10.00, then you would sell it for $20.00 (100% markup on purchase, or 50% on selling). You can obtain the latest prices for items from websites and current catalogs. You should also include what your potential profit on these items will be. Your profit will vary depending on local market demand for your products, sales volumes for a particular product, and wholesale costs. See section 6.3 for more about how to determine retail prices and track profitability for your merchandise.

Management and Staff

This section should highlight your background and business experience. This is also a good place to explain your passion for what you will be selling. You are selling yourself in this section. List any type of business background, from working in retail to relevant classes you have taken.

This section also includes information about staffing. It is unlikely you can do all the work yourself. Even if you do not plan to hire others right away, you should have a contingency plan in case you are ill, or some other catastrophe strikes. At the very least, you should make it clear you have several family members or friends willing to step in and help in case of an emergency. If you do plan to hire staff, then state that here, and mention your projected labor costs.

Financial Statements

This is the bottom line that most banks and investors will want to see. This will include start-up budgets, an estimation of revenue and expenses and a projection of when profitability will occur. See section 5.4 for more information on creating financial statements and details about financial planning for your business.

3.4.2 Start-Up Financial Planning

In the next section, you'll find a sample business plan for a new retail store. It includes samples of financial statements, including cash flow and income statements and a balance sheet. Before you look at those, let's examine the basics of financial planning and how it affects the success of your business when you're starting out.

Financial management is crucial to running a successful business. One of the first important questions you should find an answer for is how you will finance your monthly expenses until you turn a profit. These ongoing monthly costs will include things like mortgage, renting or leasing costs; employee wages; utilities, store supplies and so on. In addition, you'll need to decide how much you will pay yourself and your staff, how much you want to save for unexpected expenses, and how much you will put back into the business to finance growth.

When writing your business plan, be realistic. It is better to overestimate costs and underestimate profit. If you make more than expected in your first few months to a year, then so much the better. You will be in great shape!

Budgeting Basics

If you have ever sat down and calculated how much money you'll need for something like the family vacation by figuring out what your income and expenses are, you already know how to budget. The most difficult part of budgeting for a business is that unlike when you work for a steady paycheck, it's more difficult to project your expected income after you pay all your expenses out of your revenues.

To clarify the situation in your business plan you will need to determine, as best you can, both your start-up costs and your operating costs. The start-up budget will include all the costs necessary to get your business up and running. Your operating costs will be all of the ongoing expenses once the business is in operation. In your planning, be clear about where the money is going and why, and explain how you came to your conclusions.

The National Ice Cream Retailers Association (NICRA) gives an estimate of $70-$150 per square foot in build costs for constructing an ice cream shop, not including equipment, at **www.nicra.org/startbus.html**. Be sure to take any construction costs into account, as well as equipment costs. NICRA also provide a list of typical equipment you will need to start with. See section 4.4 for more on the topic of equipment.

When you're starting out, having a buffer of at least six months' finances available to cover your basic expenses is a good idea if you can manage it, just in case the business does not create a profit immediately. Many businesses will take up to a year to see a profit. Your store may show a profit sooner, but it's best to be prepared. In the cash flow projections in the sample business plan coming up in section 3.4.3, you will see that the company starts out with $56,000 cash on hand. This comes from the owner's cash savings and partly from an expected loan. The $56,000 helps to get the business started, although the company finishes the first six-month period with a loss of $847. You'll notice that its total expenses for the period were almost $60,000 plus start-up costs. As you can see, an initial boost that covers the start-up costs and ongoing expenses would be a great help. Here are some things you should consider when completing your revenue forecast and financial projections:

- Market trends and cycles
- Any seasonality of the business
- Varied sources of revenue
- Holidays (note that in the sample plan, revenues for summer were projected as being higher than the months before and after)
- Unexpected events (such as equipment breakdowns, personal illness, etc.)
- How will you monitor your cash flow?

The financial section of your business plan will include your financial projections, break-even analysis, a projected profit and loss statement (also called an income statement), and information about your personal finances. List expected profits and/or losses for at least the first year, but preferably for three years. You will want to break this down on a month-to-month basis. Show where the money is going and how much you expect will come in. If the business plan is for a loan, explain how much you need to borrow, why you need that much (exact uses of money), and where you plan to obtain it.

Remember to include the following items in your budgets. Notice that some expenses overlap on the start-up and operating budgets.

- *Start-up budget:* Legal and professional fees, licenses and permits, equipment, insurance, supplies, marketing costs, accounting expenses, utilities, payroll expenses.
- *Operating budget:* Make a month to month budget for at least your first year of operations, including expenses such as: staff (even if it's only your salary), insurance, rent, loan payments, advertising and promotions, legal and accounting fees, supplies, utilities, dues and subscriptions, fees, taxes and maintenance.

Sample Start-up Budget Amounts

The following is an example of a start-up budget to open a hypothetical soft-serve ice cream shop.

Item	**Low**	**High**
Rent	$2,000	$10,000
Remodeling/Improvements	10,000	70,000
Equipment	18,000	50,000
Furniture	5,000	20,000
Lighting and Fixtures	2,000	10,000
Signs	3,500	6,000
Computer Equipment	3,000	5,000
Inventory, Supplies	3,000	10,000
Insurance (first qtr.)	1,500	4,000
Loan Fees	1,500	4,000
Incorporation	500	15,000
Licenses, Permits	1,000	3,700
Supplies, Misc.	3,000	5,000
Training Expenses	1,000	3,500
Advertising	1,000	3,000
Working Capital	5,000	50,000
TOTAL:	**$61,000**	**$255,700**

You can get a good idea for the cost of many of these budget items by browsing business supply websites, talking with realtors for rental costs, and basing your wages at minimum hourly wage to start. You may want to pay higher than minimum wage to your staff in order to get more qualified employees. At times, you may have to make an educated guess based upon your research and your chats with other business owners.

Estimating Your Revenues

Depending on your geographic location, your revenues can be in the tens to the hundreds of thousands. Of course, this amount also varies greatly depending upon the demand for your products, what you pay to your suppliers, and how much you market your business.

Speak with other store owners in your general region of the country who are not competition for you. If you live in Indiana, consult with storeowners in Ohio, Illinois and Kentucky. If you live in California, consult with store owners up the coast, in Oregon or Washington, for example. If you live in New York, consult with owners in New Jersey.

One way to figure out how much you will need to sell to make a profit is to figure out the average cost of your items. (We'll look at how to figure out a break-even point based on your estimated expenses, including inventory, a little later in this section.) Depending on the suppliers you will deal with, you might be able to get a copy of a wholesale catalogue or get access to wholesale prices on the supplier's website. You may have to open a merchant account with them first, though. Once you have done a little research on who your suppliers will be, you can go ahead and contact them to get more information about your initial inventory costs.

Sales Projections

Before you can start your budget, you must arrive at some reasonable monthly sales projections. Many business decisions will be based on the level of sales that you forecast, so if you're too optimistic, you might find your business in trouble. As mentioned earlier, it's always best to be conservative in your estimates.

Alternatively, if you underestimate the amount of sales, you might make decisions that hold back the growth of your business, such as deciding on a less-than-perfect store location because the rent or building purchase price is cheaper. A certain amount of "guesstimating" is required, but you can learn as much as possible about your market beforehand in order to make the estimates more accurate.

There are two types of revenue forecasting methods: Top Down Method and Bottom Up Method.

Top Down

The Top Down Method is what retail operations most frequently use because you can fairly accurately estimate your total market size and from that the amount of money you can reasonably expect to earn from sales. To use the Top Down Method you must first estimate what the total sales potential would be. This type of information often can be gathered through the Chamber of Commerce, government census data, or from local, state, or national retailers' organizations. Then, by estimating what share of that market you can reasonably expect, you arrive at your possible sales for the year.

Calculation for Top Down Forecasting

Step 1: Total market size x average annual spending (by customers in businesses like yours) per family or per person = total market potential

Step 2: Total market potential (from Step 1) x number of competitors = average market share

Step 3: Average market share (from Step 2) x your estimated percentage of market share = potential annual sales

Bottom Up

The Bottom Up Method is most often used when forecasting revenues from delivering a service. Depending on your business, you might need to use both Top Down and Bottom Up.

The Bottom Up Method is what you will use to calculate revenues from offering services only. Service revenues are limited by the number of hours you can reasonably work. You must first calculate your rate per hour (if you have several services you're offering, use an average price per hour and average production time to make the calculations easier).

Calculation for Bottom Up Forecasting

Step 1: Hourly rate x number of hours available to work in a day = average daily sales

Step 2: Average daily sales (from Step 1) x number of days you can work per year = possible annual sales

Step 3: Possible annual sales (from Step 2) x expected rate of efficiency = projected annual sales.

NOTE: Rate of efficiency is usually about 50% in the first year. Any guaranteed contracts would have a 100% efficiency rate.

Operating Budgets

The first step in creating an operating budget is to determine what your monthly costs are. Take any bills, such as insurance and taxes, that occur either quarterly or yearly, and divide them by 4 (quarterly) or 12 (yearly) to find out how much you pay for those expenses each month.

Sample Budget Analysis for an Ice Cream Shop

Step 1: Data collected for the year projections

Description	Expenses	Revenues
Yearly projected revenue		$112,500
Lease	22,200	
Wages	18,000	
Loan repayments	8,000	
Office expenses	1,400	
Utilities	3,600	
Cost of Goods Sold*	27,900	
Taxes and membership fees	3,000	
Equipment & maintenance	5,000	
Advertising	4,425	
Totals	$93,525	$112,500
Yearly Net Profit – $18,975		

Step 2: Monthly Budget Analysis

Description	Expenses	Revenues
Yearly projected revenue		$9,375
Lease	1,850	
Wages	1,500	
Loan repayments	667	
Office Expenses	117	
Utilities	300	
Cost of Goods Sold*	2,325	
Taxes and membership fees	250	
Equipment & maintenance	417	
Advertising	369	
Totals	$7,795	$9,375
		Monthly Net Profit = $1,580

NOTE: The accounting definition of Cost of Goods Sold (COGS) is: opening inventory + cost of purchases – closing inventory. If you use inventory tracking software, you can get a good idea of your COGS on an ongoing basis, although this is not as accurate as doing regular physical inventory counts.

With these annual and average monthly figures projected, the retail owner can now take a look at where the money is being spent and make some informed decisions about how to cut back on some of the expenditures in order to grow profits. Coming up, we'll show you how to calculate a break-even point for your retail business based on the projections you have already made for your operating expenses.

If you'd like more information about budgeting for your business, check out the article, "Basic Budgets for Profit Planning", on the U.S. Small Business Administration website. The web page address is **www.sba.gov/idc/groups/public/documents/sba_homepage/pub_fm8.pdf**.

TIP: Every month, take a look at your expenditures and your sales, and update your budget and financial statements. A large setback, say purchasing inventory that doesn't sell well, or a repair to your vehicle, will mean you must redo your projections and budgets.

Calculating Your Break-Even Point

Break-even analysis is a good way to find out how much you must sell in order to cover your costs. (You can compare the result with your projected revenues to see how they match up.) This is without profit or loss; profit comes after the break-even point. Figuring out your break-even point involves a fairly straightforward calculation. You must, however, have all the figures ready in advance before you can get an accurate number. In addition, in order to calculate the break-even point, you'll first need to break out fixed (non-controllable) costs like rent from variable costs like supplies.

Sample Break-Even Point

The formula is:

$$\text{Break-even point} = \text{Total fixed costs} \div (1 - \text{total variable costs} \div \text{revenues})$$

Using the numbers from the sample budget analysis we did earlier, let's say your store has fixed expenses of $22,200 for lease payments and $8,000 for loan costs (totaling $30,200) during the first year. The rest of the budget expenses are variable costs, totaling $63,325. Based on revenues, variable costs are 56% (or in other words, for every dollar in sales, 56 cents is variable costs). Here's how to calculate your break-even point:

Break-even point = Fixed costs [$30,200] divided by (1 minus variable costs [$63,325] divided by revenues [$112,500])

30,200 ÷ (1 - 63,325 ÷ 112,500)

30,200 ÷ (1 - 0.56)

30,200 ÷ 0.44

Break-even point = $69,000 (rounded)

The store will have to earn gross revenues of about $69,000 each year in order to meet its break even point. This company is operating at 112500 ÷ 69000 or 163% of break-even, meaning it is profitable. With these figures determined, you can now look at ways of reducing your variable costs as well as increasing your revenues to try to widen the gap between gross revenues and your break-even point. It's also a good way to see if your projected revenues are realistic when balanced against known expenses.

When Can You Expect to Turn a Profit?

This varies widely from region to region, store to store, and owner to owner. Most stores break even sometime during the first year. You can reasonably expect to start making profits after that time period.

A lot will also depend on your overhead costs. If you are running a high volume shop with low overhead costs, you may turn a profit very quickly.

One idea might be to start small with a limited menu selection and with a low square footage and then move to a larger space as your business grows. This way, you'll see a profit much quicker without the risk involved in investing your own or someone else's money.

3.4.3 A Sample Business Plan

Keep in mind that this is a somewhat simplified business plan. You will need to provide more detailed information in some areas, particularly in the financial section (including financial statements) of your plan.

Sample Business Plan: YoDazzle

Cover Page

Include the title, your name and contact information.

Executive Summary

YoDazzle is an exciting new concept in the ice cream and frozen desserts industry. While many ice cream shops exist, there are no retailers offering premium frozen yogurt or specializing in frozen yogurt in our immediate community. While a frozen yogurt craze has been sweeping the West Coast and other parts of the United States, it has yet to reach our part of the country. By offering a unique product made of the finest ingredients in a café-like environment, I plan to generate the same buzz and popularity that is creating a cult-like following elsewhere.

Our shop will sell nonfat frozen yogurt in three flavors with a variety of toppings. Menu items will include frozen yogurt served in bowls, as Dazzlers, a blended yogurt drink, and parfaits. Focusing on a limited selection will establish the store's identity and strengthen its reputation as the prime place to go for the best frozen yogurt. As the store becomes established, we will explore adding additional items, such as smoothies and frozen ices, to our product selection as driven by the demands of our clientele.

Start-up date for the store has been set for May 1 of this year, which is a few weeks before the summer selling season and start of the busiest tourist period. We will be located at 1099 Riverfront Dr., Holidaytown, SC (population 80,000). This location is excellent due to its proximity to both tourist attractions and the downtown business area. In addition, it is within walking distance of two local colleges (total student population of 25,000) and a residential area of upper-income residents. There is heavy pedestrian traffic as well as a nearby municipal parking lot. There are no other carryout frozen dessert shops in the immediate area, despite its high concentration of retail businesses and high draw for shoppers and tourists.

The store will be managed by owner Ima Yogurtseller. Ms. Yogurtseller has 14 years' experience in the food industry, including working as an assistant manager in an ice cream shop in Travel Town, NC. In addition, she has completed a number of continuing education courses, including course in entrepreneurship, marketing, bookkeeping and accounting, as well as an ice cream retailers seminar. Assistant manager, Iluva Treat, who has been in frozen desserts retail sales for more than 10 years, will provide additional management experience. The store will hire part-time staff as required and as growth allows.

The store can be operated with a minimum of staff, requiring only four or five personnel during the busiest of times, and one or two at others. As the menu will be highly select and limited, inventory tracking and ordering will be simple and effective.

With only four other ice cream and frozen desserts stores located within the city limits and no other frozen yogurt store in the wider metropolitan area, we expect to turn a profit within the first year of operations. We estimate that with the high volume of tourists, college students, nearby high-income residents, and downtown district employees and the lack of immediate competition, coupled with our unique product offering, we will capture approximately 10-20% of the local ice cream and frozen dessert market in the first year. This translates to more than $100,000 in sales.

Both the location and the timing are perfect for starting this type of business in our community. We have identified a lucrative market niche that has gone unfilled before now. No other frozen dessert outlet in the area offers the products that we do. With the extensive experience and savvy business acumen of its management, YoDazzle will be one of the most profitable frozen desserts retail ventures in the area.

Table of Contents

To be completed last.

Description of the Business

YoDazzle will be a frozen yogurt shop offering nonfat frozen yogurt with a variety of unique toppings for people of all ages in a contemporary and innovative atmosphere. Frozen yogurt mix will come from YoYo Suppliers and toppings from Novel Toppings.

Our goals by the end of the year are to be profitable and to be one of the top three destinations of choice for frozen desserts in Holidaytown.

The store will be open seven days a week, starting on May 1 this year, from 11:00 a.m. to 11:00 p.m. It will offer the following menu items:

- Nonfat frozen yogurt made from a dry mix and water. The frozen yogurt will have active and live culture colonies and meet the standards of the National Yogurt Association to be identified as yogurt rather than a similar product with low or no active culture colonies.

- Frozen yogurt will come in three flavors: a tart vanilla, chocolate, and Asian tea.

- Frozen yogurt will be sold by the bowl, as a blended drink, and as a parfait. Bowls will come in three sizes: small (8 oz.), medium (10 oz.), and large (12 oz.), with a variety of topping options. The blended drink, called a Dazzler, will consist of frozen yogurt and toppings blended together, and will come in two sizes: medium and large. The parfait will consist of layered frozen yogurt and fruit topped by granola. Parfaits will come in two sizes: medium and large.

- Toppings, called dazzles, of fruit, nuts, cereal, and candy. Initial toppings will be strawberries, blueberries, raspberries, mango, kiwi, cherries, peaches, granola, walnuts, caramelized pecans, hazelnuts, yogurt drops, carob drops, shaved chocolate, chocolate chips, mint chocolate chips, shaved coconut, gummy bears, Oreo cookies, maple candy bits, honey drops, and citrus candy slices.

In addition to its unique product offerings, the store will distinguish itself from other frozen desserts shops and create its own unique identity by the following:

- The store's interior will be designed to create a modernistic but minimalist environment that creates a sense of a luxury boutique-like cafe. Walls will be a stark white tile with green trim. One wall will contain a large Photo Board of photographs of actual customers. Furniture will incorporate simple aesthetics, curved lines, and lightly tinted materials.

- An LCD Video monitor mounted on the back wall behind the serving area will display dynamic images of frozen yogurt concoctions, the dazzles (toppings), customers eating YoDazzle frozen yogurt, and abstract backgrounds. The images will be synchronized with the melody and rhythm of New Age music playing softly in the background.

- The LCD Video monitor will be programmed to "burst" into a dazzle of images at random intervals. The images on the video will gradually fade out to a black background speckled with galaxy-like stars and then erupt into a dramatic and dazzling display of fireworks. The music will change to signal the onset of the 15-second light show. At the conclusion of the light show, the words "Be Dazzled" will appear. Customers at the counter who are in the process of placing an order at the time the light show starts will "be dazzled" and select a Be Dazzled promotional card from a bowl. Cards will offer a variety of promotions, such as a free yogurt with toppings, free topping, 10% off, and free order.

- Staff will photograph customers eating yogurt and winning Be Dazzled cards to display on the Photo Board and in the LED Video presentation.

The store will be approximately 1,000 to 1,200 square feet in area. Approximately 45 percent of the floor space will be dedicated to the customer-seating area, about 35 percent to the serving area, and check-out areas, and 20 percent to the storage area and back office.

Customer seats will be located at the front of the store along both walls so that customers can sit and enjoy their yogurt after ordering. By placing the seating area near the serving area and line, it is hoped that patrons will relax to eat without lingering for an extended period.

There will be one serving counter with two stations to allow for two lines of customers. Each station will have a server and cashier. The cashiers will be in the center of the counter, with each serving station to the left or right. The serving area will be located far enough from the front door to prevent customer lineups blocking the entry. A private area at the rear of the store will include a small storage space, staff washroom, and owner's office.

Description of the Industry

The frozen yogurt segment of the ice cream and frozen desserts industry is experiencing a renaissance. Highly popular in the 1980s and early 1990s, sales of frozen yogurt took a sleep decline in 1996, which continued for many years. Interest in frozen yogurt picked up with the advent of several frozen yogurt shops in the Los Angeles, California area, with imitators opening up similar shops and franchises spreading to other locations. According to the U.S. Department of Agriculture's National Agricultural Statistics Service, in 2006 Americans spent $1.2 billion on soft frozen yogurt purchases to eat away from home. Although frozen yogurt remains a relatively small segment of the total ~$23 billion ice cream industry, it is growing, with a sales gain of 2% in total sales in 2006 over 2005.

Frozen yogurt fills a niche desired by consumers. Many consumers are seeking healthy, lowfat or nonfat alternatives to ice cream but want to retain the taste of higher-fat products. Frozen yogurt satisfies this desire by providing a rich, creamy frozen product low in calories without sacrificing taste. Likewise, consumers want to customize their desserts, as evidenced by the growing popularity of mix-in ingredients and toppings. And consumers crave gourmet or specialty items, such as exotic nuts and fresh fruits. YoDazzle's toppings will allow customers to create frozen indulgences based on individual taste preferences. Customers can select gourmet items such as hazelnuts or more traditional fares such as chocolate chips.

The industry appears to be perched at a point where the sales of frozen yogurt could rapidly escalate. YoDazzle wants to be at the forefront of this trend and thus grab a larger slice of the market share. With no nearby competitor offering a similar product, YoDazzle will gain a foothold in this emerging subsection of the ice cream and frozen desserts industry and establish itself as the market leader. Through promotion and reputation, YoDazzle hopes to increase the consumption of frozen yogurt, which currently averages about one pound per person per year.

YoDazzle believes that customers will be willing to spend between $4 and $7 for frozen yogurt bowls, drinks, and parfaits based on competitor pricing of similar items made with super-premium ice cream. According to *Ice Cream World*, the industry's leading trade publication, the average price for one scoop of super-premium ice cream with two mix-ins was $6.50 in 2007. This is significantly higher than our medium sized bowl of frozen yogurt, priced at $4.99.

Given that our community has a high number of tourists (1.2 million annually) who spend an average of $60 a day on food purchases during their visits (per the Holidaytown Chamber of Commerce), and the relatively high incomes of the residents in the surrounding area ($76,770, per the 2006 American Community Survey, US Census Bureau), customers in this area have demonstrated a willingness to pay high prices for eating snack foods away from home.

> (**Ice Cream World* is a fictional publication for this example. A real business plan needs real data sources, which you can find online through resources such as the U.S. Census report on Statistics of U.S. Businesses at **www.census.gov/csd/susb/susb.htm** or through industry magazines and organizational reports. Each industry has its own organization.)

Business Legal Structure

Limited Liability Corporation (LLC). We have chosen the LLC business legal structure because it allows the freedom of running the business as a sole proprietorship and simplifies tax returns while still protecting person assets. *(*Note to reader: This may not be the best choice for you. Please read section 3.6.1 on legal structure and consult with a lawyer or other professional, if you are still uncertain.)*

Business Location

A 1,200 square foot space located on Riverfront Dr. is currently available for lease. The location borders the high-traffic downtown corridor, historic resident district, and waterfront area. Several visitor attractions are nearby, including the ocean and beach, visitors center, pier, park, jogging path, historic walking path, tour boats, military museum, children's center, and historic churches and buildings. A municipal parking lot is within a short walking distance. The location is also served by the visitors' trolley operated by the city's visitor center.

The location formerly housed a fast-foods operation and is equipped with a walk-in freezer as well as a refrigerator. The layout lends itself to the proposed layout of YoDazzle, although the interior will need to be remodeled and redecorated. The back area, or employees' area, which will contain areas for food storage and refrigeration, an employee washroom, and small office, can be retained with minimal changes. The customer area will need to have new ceramic walls and floors installed as well as a serving counter, furniture, and other furnishings. A neon sign will be attached to the inside of the window, showing the shop's logo, which will consist of the word YoDazzle above an arc ending in a burst of firework shaped lines, with a sprinkle of tiny star-shaped objects scattered below like confetti. The words "Get Dazzled" will extend in smaller type below the arc.

Target Market

The products will be marketed to visitors, college students, local residents, and residents in the greater metropolitan area. The area is a noted tourist destination, attracting approximately 1.2 million visitors a year. Visitors include both families and older couples, as well as college-age students on spring break and other holidays. There is a significant college-age population, with 7 colleges and universities within a 25-mile radius. The college-age population has not been included in the projected sales estimates, although we do aim to market sales toward this group.

Anticipating sales to this group is difficult due to fluctuations in the number of students throughout the year, limited spending in comparison to other groups, and tendency of this group to stay relatively close to restaurants in strips bordering the college campuses. Visitors spend on average $30 a day on food. Impulse food purchases are high, with the majority of nearby fast-food businesses showing high profits. Local residents in the immediate area consist of families and a high number of baby boomers—both single individuals and married couples. Households in this area have above-average incomes, with an average income of $76,770. Baby boomers and affluent consumers have demonstrated an above-average consumption of gourmet treats such as super-premium ice cream, and we aim to capture at least 20% of this market group.

We expect at least one purchase by at least 1% of the visiting population for total annual sales of $50,000 to $60,000. Adding in anticipated sales of 1-3 purchases by 20% of the residents of Holidaytown boosts overall projections by $80,000-$240,000, for potential annual sales of $130,000 - $300,000 sales per year.

We can capture at least 10% of this market with targeted advertising and word-of-mouth business. We aim to capture an even greater share of 20% in the first five years, with additional gains in subsequent years.

Inventory and Pricing

Starting inventory will be purchased from YoYo Suppliers, Candy Accessories, Fruit & More, and Novel Toppings. Retention of suppliers will be determined by customer preferences and future trends, with new suppliers obtained if necessary.

Pricing for each menu item is as follows:

- *Frozen yogurt bowls with one topping:* small - $3.99; medium - $4.99; large - $5.99
- *Extra toppings* - $0.99 each
- *Dazzlers:* medium - $5.45; large - $6.95
- *Parfaits:* medium - $5.95; large - $6.95

Promotion

We will run advertising in the local newspapers, visitor guide, and other tourist brochures; distribute promotional coupons to hotels, restaurants, and tourist venues; and send invitations/announcements to select residences in neighboring communities announcing the grand opening. The in-store Be Dazzled activity will encourage return visits with the awarding of coupons and other promotions to winners of random drawings.

Competition

While there are three ice cream and frozen dessert shops in the city borders, none of them is selling frozen yogurt. However, YoDazzle will be vying for the same customers as these shops. Two of the shops are combination restaurant-ice cream parlors offering extended service to patrons and offer no direct competition to YoDazzle. The third shop, Soft Whirls, is most similar to YoDazzle, targeting walk-in, quick-serve customers, and is the only real competition in the frozen dessert market. Soft Whirls sells soft serve ice cream with traditional toppings such as cookies, candies, and nuts. It opened approximately seven years ago and with minimal advertising has developed a customer base of nearly 16,000 people (a 20% market share of the city's year-round population). However, it does not have promotional strategies such as in-store events, and its products are not perceived as gourmet, or high-end, items.

Other ice cream and frozen dessert shops beyond the city borders and tourist area are primarily sit-down, casual-service food establishments or are located so far away that they cannot be considered competition. Indirect competitors include restaurants with dessert items on the menu. However, these only compete against us for a different type of customer, and thus it is not anticipated that they will significantly impact our market share.

Table 1: Competitor Analysis

YoDazzle	Strength/ Weakness	Competitor: Soft Whirls	Importance to Customer
PRODUCTS			
Higher quality	Strength	Much less	High
PRICE			
Higher price	Weakness	Much less	Medium
QUALITY			
High	Strength	Much less	Medium
SELECTION			
Smaller	Weakness	More	Medium

YoDazzle	Strength/ Weakness	Competitor: Soft Whirls	Importance to Customer
Service			
Excellent service with a smile	Strength	Service okay	Medium
Reliability			
Extremely reliable	Strength	Reliable	Medium
Stability			
Low - if we do not do well, we will eventually close	Weakness	Very stable and established. This is a real strength of theirs.	Medium
Expertise			
Very high	Strength	High	Medium
Company Reputation			
N/A		High	Medium
Location			
Prime location with lots of traffic	Strength	Good location. Less traffic.	High
Appearance			
Professional and neat. Well organized.	Strength	Same	Medium
Sales Method			
Targeted advertising	Strength	Targeted advertising	Medium
Credit Policies			
Accept cards, cash or check	Strength	Same	High
Advertising			
Planning a lot of ads in different media	Strength	Does some advertising	Medium
Image			
N/A	Weakness	Good	Medium

Management and Staff

The owner and manager of YoDazzle will be Ima Yogurtseller. Ima Yogurtseller has worked in the retail food industry for many years and has helped to launch a new ice cream shop in a resort town in North Carolina. As the assistant manager, she helped design the shop, select vendors, hire and train employees, run the advertising campaign, and develop relationships with the community. Within six months, the shop was turning a profit, and today it has annual sales of over $800,000.

Ima Yogurtseller has attended several national and regional trade conventions and successfully completed the highly acclaimed Penn State ice cream course. Her insider knowledge of how the ice cream and frozen desserts industry works combined with awareness of what customers want and need will create success. She has strong business skills, a strong sense of market demand, and the ability to transform ideas into action. Combined with her organizational and leadership expertise, she has the experience and professional skills necessary to operate and market YoDazzle in a professional and profitable manner.

Iluva Treat, with more than 10 years' experience in frozen desserts retail sales worked with Ima Yogurtseller in the aforementioned ice cream shop in North Carolina. Starting as a line server during the summer, she advanced to purchasing and marketing positions within the store. Iluva Treat will work approximately 34 to 40 hours per week at a starting wage of $10/hour. Ima Yogurtseller will receive no salary during the first year, but will take draws when feasible. She expects to take a $45,000 annual salary in subsequent years when the store is profitable. Additional staffing will be provided by family members and local college students hired on a part-time, as-needed basis.

Financial Information

Risks

As with any business venture there are risks associated with opening this frozen yogurt shop. One possibility is that our main competitor,

Soft Whirls, might decide to start selling frozen yogurt. However, we see this as a remote possibility as it would negate its existing customer base, who have shown a preference for soft-serve ice cream. In addition, Soft Whirls's current products are priced lower than YoDazzle's will be, and it does not target customers seeking high-quality, premium products. Even if it were to offer frozen yogurt, it is unlikely that it would offer the same quality of product or variety of gourmet toppings.

Another risk might be that a new frozen yogurt shop might open in the area. This could pose a very real threat, particularly if it offered a similar high-quality product. By opening first, YoDazzle hopes to develop identity and product awareness, thus giving it an edge should another similar store appear on the scene. In addition, the store's environment will create a unique setting that will attract customers looking for a unique place to enjoy their frozen dessert treats. By positing itself as innovative and by establishing an outstanding reputation, YoDazzle will retain its original customer base and minimize any threat to sales by any potential competitors.

We believe that our sales targets are realistic based on our market research, but there is always the possibility that our target sales will not be achieved for the year. We will closely monitor revenues on a daily, weekly and monthly basis to ensure that our sales targets are being reached, and if they are not, we will make every effort to discover why not and correct any issues we discover. Start-up capital will carry the store's expenses through the first six months of operations.

> [You should include any additional risks that you can think of that might affect your business.]

Cash Flow

Excluding the spike in cash flow for holiday sales increases, we project positive cash flow beginning in April of next year. Following are our cash flow projections for the first two quarterly periods of operations (note that these figures include sales projections for the first six months of operations starting in May):

YoDazzle Cash Flow Projections – 1st 6 Months of Operations

	May	Jun	Jul	Aug	Sep	Oct
Cash on Hand	$56,000	$2,545	$571	-$716	$261	-$884
Sales Revenues	$6,500	$7,150	$9,295	$12,084	$7,865	$8,652
Total Cash & Sales	$62,500	$9,695	$9,866	$11,368	$8,126	$7,768
Start-up expenses						
Remodeling	$10,000					
Fixtures/ Furniture	$7,000					
Equipment/ Supplies	$18,000					
Uniforms	$700					
Inventory	$3,000					
Licenses	$1,000					
Legal & Accounting	$1,300					
Signage & Logo	$3,500					
Computer & Office Supplies	$3,000					
Website Design	$1,000					
Total Start-Up Costs	**$48,500**					

	May	Jun	Jul	Aug	Sep	Oct
Ongoing Expenses						
Rent	$1,200	$600	$600	$600	$600	$600
Inventory/ Supplies	$1,300	$1,430	$1,859	$2,417	$1,573	$1,730
Advertising/ Promotion	$1,500	$800	$1,000	$800	$200	$200
Accounting	$300	$150	$150	$150	$150	$150
Legal	$600	$200	$200	$200	$200	$200
Telephone	$120	$120	$120	$120	$120	$120
Utilities	$1,200	$1,400	$1,700	$1,700	$1,700	$1,400
Maintenance & Repair Service	$310	$310	$310	$310	$310	$310
Website Maintenance	$240	$240	$240	$240	$240	$240
Wages	$2,500	$1,800	$2,200	$2,200	$1,800	$1,500
Taxes	$390	$429	$558	$725	$472	$519
Insurance	$620	$620	$620	$620	$620	$620
Office Supplies	$250	$100	$100	$100	$100	$100
Loan Repayment	$925	$925	$925	$925	$925	$925
Total Ongoing Expenses	**$11,455**	**$9,124**	**$10,582**	**$11,107**	**$9,010**	**$8,614**
Total Expenses	**$59,955**	**$9,124**	**$10,582**	**$11,107**	**$9,010**	**$8,614**
Cash Ending	**$2,545**	**$571**	**-$716**	**$261**	**$-884**	**$-847**

[You should create a month by month cash flow projection sheet for the entire year to include in your business plan, rather than the six months in our example.]

Statement of Personal Assets

Following is the statement of personal assets of Ima Yogurtseller.

Personal Assets & Liabilities of Ima Yogurtseller

ASSETS	
Current Assets	
Cash	$1,000
Investments (401K)	$55,000
Total Current Assets	**$56,000**
Long-Term Assets	
Automobile	$12,500
Home Equity	$125,000
Total Long-term Assets	$137,500
Total Assets	**$291,550**

LIABILITIES	
Current Liabilities	
Car Loan Payment	$400
Mortgage Payment	$650
Utilities and Other Expenses	$750
Property Taxes	$1,500
Total Current Liabilities	$33,000
Long-Term Liabilities	
Car Loan	$9,000
Mortgage	$150,000
Total Long-term Liabilities	$159,000
Total Liabilities	**$162,300**

Total Net Assets	**$31,200**

[For a start-up company, one without business assets and liabilities, you should create a statement like this to represent the owner(s) total personal assets and liabilities.]

YoDazzle Income Statement Projections – 1st 6 Months of Operations

	May	Jun	Jul	Aug	Sep	Oct
Revenues						
Cash Sales	$5,525	$6,078	$7,901	$10,271	$3,275	$2,952
Credit Card Sales	$975	$1,073	$1,394	$1,813	$4,590	$5,700
Total Cash & Sales	$6,500	$7,150	$9,295	$12,084	$7,865	$8,652
Expenses						
Controllable Expenses						
Cost of Goods Sold	$1,700	$1,570	$1,141	$583	$1,427	$1,270
Wages	$2,500	$1,800	$2,200	$2,200	$1,800	$1,500
Office Supplies	$250	$100	$100	$100	$100	$100
Advertising/ Promotion	$1,500	$800	$1,000	$800	$200	$200
Utilities	$1,200	$1,400	$1,700	$1,700	$1,700	$1,400
Accounting	$300	$150	$150	$150	$150	$150
Legal	$600	$200	$200	$200	$200	$200
Total Controllable Expenses	**$8,050**	**$6,020**	**$6,491**	**$5,733**	**$5,577**	**$4,820**
Gross Profit/Loss	**-$1,550**	**$1,130**	**$2,804**	**$6,351**	**$2,288**	**$3,832**

YoDazzle Income Statement Projections – 1st 6 Months of Operations (continued)

	MAY	JUN	JUL	AUG	SEP	OCT
Fixed Expenses						
Rent	$1,200	$600	$600	$600	$600	$600
Telephone	$120	$120	$120	$120	$120	$120
Website	$240	$240	$240	$240	$240	$240
Maintenance & Repair Service	$310	$310	$310	$310	$310	$310
Loan Repayment	$925	$925	$925	$925	$925	$925
Depreciation	$150	$151	$152	$153	$154	$155
Insurance	$620	$620	$620	$620	$620	$620
Total Non-Controllable Expenses	**$3,565**	**$2,966**	**$2,967**	**$2,968**	**$2,969**	**$2,970**
Net Income Before Taxes	**-$5,115**	**$1,836**	**-$163**	**$3,383**	**-$681**	**$862**
Taxes	0	0	0	$677	0	$172

NET INCOME	**($5,115)**	**($1,836)**	**($163)**	**$4,059**	**($681)**	**$1,034**

[As with the Cash Flow Projections sheet earlier in this section, you should create monthly income statements for at least the entire first year.]

Other Items

In addition to the items listed above, your business plan might include things such as a statement of personal finances (this can include a print-out of your credit history and tax returns), a resume, reference letters, and other items. It is up to you if you want to include these things. Always err on the side of giving more information, especially if you are unsure if you can secure a loan based on the information you're providing to lenders.

Another item you might want to add is a loan proposal or request for funding. In the example financial statements above, the owner has borrowed against the $55,000 in a 401K to add to the owner's $1,000 cash in order to carry the business through the first six months of operations. A lender or investor will want to see a loan proposal or request for funding detailing how much money you want to borrow, what you plan to spend the money on, and how you plan to pay it back.

Under this heading, state the amount of money you are asking for, whether it is a debt or equity funding request (i.e. if you are borrowing money, that is debt funding; if you are asking someone to invest in your business as a shareholder or minority partner, that is equity funding), how you plan to repay a loan, or what an investor gets out of investing in your company. You loan proposal should include:

- How much money you want
- How long it take you to pay it back
- Details of how you plan to spend the money
- How you will get the money to pay back the loan
- A description of your own personal assets and other collateral that you can use to secure the loan

If your business will need start-up financing the next section will tell you how to go about finding it.

3.4.4 Business Plan Resources

You can find a free sample business for a frozen custard business, which shares many similarities with a typical fast-food ice cream shop, at **www.bplans.com/frozen_custard_shop_business_plan/executive_summary_fc.cfm**.

Here are some additional resources that you might find useful in helping you to write your business plan:

- *SBA: Writing the Plan*
  www.sba.gov/smallbusinessplanner/plan/writeabusinessplan/index.html

- *SCORE: Business Plan Templates*
  www.score.org/template_gallery.html

- *Canada Business: Business Planning*
  www.canadabusiness.ca/eng/86/

- *BDC (Canada) Business Plan Template*
  www.bdc.ca/en/business_tools/business_plan/default.htm

TIP: When writing your business plan, pay close attention to spelling and grammar, and try to write clearly and concisely. You don't want to make reading the plan a chore.

3.5 Start-Up Financing

This section covers sources of start-up financing, and what you'll need to present to lenders in order to apply for funding. Additional advice on all aspects of financing your business can be found at the SBA's Small Business Planner website at **www.sba.gov/smallbusinessplanner** (under "Start Your Business", click on "Finance Start-Up" then choose "Financing Basics"). In Canada, visit **www.canadabusiness.ca/eng/125/142**.

3.5.1 Getting Prepared

When looking for funding, you must first be well prepared before approaching any potential loan or investment sources. You will need the following things:

- *A Business Plan:* As you learned in the previous section, a business plan is the document that lenders will review to decide whether or not to give you a loan. This document is absolutely necessary for banks or other lenders, and even if you are getting the start-up money you need from a rich aunt, you should prepare your business plan and present it so the person lending you money can see that you have a clear and organized plan. (If you haven't read it already, see section 3.4 for advice on creating a business plan.) Your financial statements are a particularly important part of your business plan.

- *A Personal Financial Statement:* This should be prepared as part of your business plan. It is important because you need to have a clear picture of your own financial state to know exactly where you are financially before you begin. This financial statement will tell you:

  - How much money you need every month to pay your bills

  - What kind of resources or assets you have

  - What kind of debt you carry. How will you repay this debt while you are putting your total effort into opening your store?

- *A Start-Up Survival Nest Egg:* Many financial consultants think that having a nest egg to live on while you are starting up your store is one of the most important things you can have. Some suggest at least six months' of living expense money — that is, all the money you will need monthly to pay all your personal living expenses, bills, and debts, so you can focus on your new retail business without stress. This is apart from any reserve start-up capital you might need for the business itself.

> *"The biggest mistake I see new ice cream franchise owners making is not having enough cash in reserve to keep them up and running for at least 3 to 5 years. You can't count on making money just because it's a franchise and you feel that you've done all your research and things are going to be great!! This isn't always the case."*
>
> — Pam Nardinelli, owner, Marble Slab Creamery

Asking for Money

Keep these tips in mind when you ask someone for funding:

- Get an introduction or referral. If you can get someone who is respected in the community to introduce you to a potential lender, it gives you credibility and that's a big advantage.
- Have an extra copy of your business plan available for the potential lender's inspection, and be able to speak clearly and concisely about your plans. Be able to discuss all aspects of your business plan, your long-range goals and your prospective market.
- Be professional. Shake hands, speak with confidence and look the person you're talking to in the eye.
- Dress to impress. You're going to be a business owner. Be sure you look the part.
- Be receptive. Even if you don't end up getting any money from a prospective lender or investor, you may be able to get ideas and suggestions from them. Perhaps they'll have some pointers regarding your business plan, or some suggestions about steering your business in a particular direction. Don't be afraid to ask questions, either.

Remember that if someone agrees to loan you money or invest in your business, they're doing so because they believe in you and what you can do. When you ask someone for money, you need to sell yourself and your ideas. Make sure you have a great sales pitch.

There are a number of online resources to help you find out more about financing options for your business. The SBA link noted above is a good place to start in the United States. In the "Start Your Business" section of the Small Business Planner, open the "Finance Start-Up" link and scroll down to find Loan and Funding information. In Canada, you can try Industry Canada's "Search for Financing" page at **www.canadabusiness.ca/eng/82**.

Now that you know the basics, you are ready to determine who you will approach for your funding.

3.5.2 Equity vs. Debt Financing

In business, there are two basic kinds of financing: equity financing and debt financing. Essentially, equity financing is when you agree to give someone a share in your business in exchange for an agreed amount of investment capital from that person. Debt financing is, as you probably already know, borrowing money at interest that you pay back in installments over time or in a lump sum at a specified future date. (Or repayment could be a combination of these; the point is, you'll pay interest). The decision to choose debt or equity financing usually will be based on your personal financial position and how much additional money you need in order to get your business started.

One form of equity financing is investment capital provided by venture capitalists. You'll want to look for an individual or investment firm that is familiar with your industry. You'll have less explaining of your business concept to do and they might be more open to investing in a company such as yours whose premise they already understand.

While a venture capital investor won't expect you to pay interest and regular monthly installments, they will expect some kind of return on their investment. This could include dividends paid out of your net income, the right to interfere with operations if they think they could do better, or the right to resell their interest to someone else for a higher price than they originally paid for their share of your company. Make sure that you are comfortable with the terms of any investment capital agreement, and that it clearly specifies what your obligations are. Check with a lawyer if you're not sure.

Another form of equity investment comes from your circle of friends and your family. You might be able to get a no-interest loan from a family member or a close friend, with the promise to pay them back at a time in the future when your business is self-sustaining. This is an ideal situation for you so long as the lender has no expectation of "helping" you run your business if you're not comfortable with that. You may also decide to bring in a friend, business acquaintance, or family member as a partner if they have some capital to invest to help cover start-up costs.

Debt financing is any form of borrowing, including a loan, lease, line of credit or other debt instrument on which you must pay interest in order to finance the original principal amount. Sources for this kind of financing include banks, credit unions, credit card companies, suppliers, and so on. If you buy a computer system for your company and pay for it in monthly installments over a couple of years, that is a form of debt financing since you will pay interest on the amount you finance. In the following sections we'll look at some of the sources of each type of financing and the advantages and disadvantages to each.

3.5.3 Borrowing Money

You can choose to utilize any mixture of the financing suggestions that follow. Many new business owners choose a mix of some of their own savings, a family loan, and a small business loan. Only you can decide which financing sources will be the best ones for your business and your personal situation. The most important thing is to make sure you agree to loan repayment terms that you can live with and that are realistic for you.

Commercial Loans

Commercial loans are loans that you can get from a financial institution like a bank or a credit union. You can go to your neighborhood bank around the corner to set up all your small business banking needs, or you can shop around for a bank that will offer you the best loan terms possible.

The terms of your loan will depend upon several things:

- Your credit score
- Your collateral
- Your ability to pay back a loan

There are a number of different loan types you can enter into with these financial institutions. They offer both long-term and short-term loans. For example, you might choose an operating term loan with a repayment period of one year. This will help you finance your start-up costs such as buying equipment and inventory or pay for any renovations you might need to do.

> **TIP:** If you're looking for a long-term loan of less than $50,000 the bank will probably consider it a personal loan. As a result, they will be more interested in your personal credit history, and they may require you to put up personal assets such as real estate as security.

You might also choose a business line of credit if your situation warrants such an arrangement. In this setup, the bank will grant you what is in essence a revolving loan in a specified amount, and will honor any checks you write to pay for your ongoing business expenses. You will pay interest on any amounts outstanding under the line of credit.

Remember that lines of credit are to be used to pay for operating expenses as needed. Don't abuse the privilege by going out and buying thousands of dollars worth of office equipment or a new car for the business. If you do, then you won't be able to meet the projections you gave the lender when you presented the business plan to them. Those projections are why you got the line of credit in the first place.

Operating term loans and lines of credit, particularly if they are unsecured by assets (or other collateral), will have higher rates of interest attached. In some cases, the lender may require that you offer some sort of security for the loan, such as having a co-signer or putting up your personal assets against it. Some lenders may accept inventory (usually at 50% of your cost to purchase it) as a portion of collateral. Another consideration is that your interest rate will change as the bank's interest rates fluctuate.

You might choose a long-term loan, rather than short-term financing, if you need to do major renovations or building, or take out a mortgage if you intend to purchase a building as your retail location. One advantage to this type of financing is that the interest rates are usually lower. This is because the loan is paid back over a longer period of time than an operating term loan or line of credit, and you pay interest at a fixed, instead of a variable, rate. Another reason interest is lower is that the loan is backed by the value of the asset you're purchasing. This makes repayment of the loan more likely. (The lender can always sell an asset like a building if you default on the loan.)

One major disadvantage to a long-term loan is that you will have a debt burden that you will need to carry for a number of years. This can affect your company's growth because you might not have the liquidity you need to pay for expansion or to pursue new lines of merchandise. You might also have to pay a financial penalty if you decide to pay back the loan earlier. Consider all your options carefully before you enter into any kind of long-term debt arrangement. Speak with an accountant and a lawyer first.

Personal Loans

One of the greatest resources for your start-up money will always be the people you know who believe in you and your ideas—your family and friends. Very often they will help you with money when all other resources fail you. They usually will agree to payback terms that aren't as strict as commercial lenders, and they are usually pulling for you, too. As with any other kind of loan, it is important to make sure that you and the other parties completely understand and agree to the terms of the loan. Also, make sure to put everything in writing.

Another possibility is to ask a family member to co-sign a commercial loan for you. Co-signing means that this person agrees to take on the financial responsibility of the loan if you should fail. Family members are often willing to help you out this way. Make sure, before friends or family members help you out by co-signing a loan, that they are really comfortable doing so.

3.5.4 Finding Investors

Venture Capital and Investment Capital Investors

Depending on the type and size of your business, you might consider finding investors to help you with your start-up capital. You find may find that some investors are not willing to invest venture capital in a small, single-location retail store, however, many small retailers have gone on to grow their companies into regional or national chains. So this type of investment may well be something you'll want to look into for the future. As you'll see later in this section, there are ways to find investors willing to put money into small businesses.

Remember that investors are looking to make money by investing their capital in your business. They may or may not be people you know, but they will want you to show them how they will make a profit by helping you. You have to assure them that they will get something out of it, because for them investing in your store isn't personal (like it might be when a family member invests in your business), it is business. Investors work one of two ways:

- They want to see their initial money returned with a profit
- They want to own part of your business

While investment capital might seem like a great idea, be aware that many entrepreneurs have been burned when venture capital vanished when the start-up money was needed. As mentioned earlier, the investment agreement could contain unsavory terms that give too great a portion of control to the investor instead of leaving it in the hands of the company owner.

However, on the plus side, private investors can be more flexible to deal with than lending institutions like banks. They may not want to get too deeply involved with the day-to-day management of the company. They might also be more willing to accept a higher level of risk than a bank, trusting in your skills and knowledge of the industry and leave your assets unencumbered.

To find venture capital investors beyond your immediate circle of family and friends, you can investigate some of the resources found at the websites listed below.

- *VFinance*
  www.vfinance.com
- *Angel Capital Association Member Directory*
  www.angelcapitalassociation.org/dir_directory/directory.aspx

- *BDC Venture Capital*
  www.bdc.ca/en/business_solutions/venture_capital/about_us/venture_capital.htm

You can also find investment capital through the Small Business Administration's Small Business Investment Company (SBIC) program. While the SBA does not act as an intermediary on behalf of entrepreneurs, they do have a wealth of information about the process of finding investors on their website at the "SBA Entrepreneurs Seeking Financing" link below. You can use their services to help you put together a business plan and a request for funding package (see more about this in section 3.5.5), which you can then submit to SBICs that might be interested in providing you with investment capital. You can search for SBICs to match your needs at **www.sba.gov/aboutsba/sbaprograms/inv/esf/INV_DIRECTORY_SBIC.html**.

- *SBA Entrepreneurs Seeking Financing*
  www.sba.gov/aboutsba/sbaprograms/inv/esf/index.html

- *PrivateEquity.com*
  (Click on "Private Equity Firms".)
  http://privateequity.com

- *The National Association of Small Business Investment Companies*
  www.nasbic.org/?page=SBIC_financing

You have to decide what you want. Do you feel you will be able to meet the investor's terms? Do you want to share ownership of your business with another person? For some new business owners, the perfect solution is to find a person who wants to partner with them, share the responsibility of their new store, and bring some money to invest.

Partners

One of the simplest forms of equity financing is taking on a partner. Having a partner in your business brings additional skill sets, business contacts and resources to the venture. Most importantly, a partner can bring money to help pay for start-up costs and assist with ongoing operations. You'll need to decide whether your partner will be active in the running of the company or just a silent partner who invests the money, receives income from the business, but has no say in how things are run. (You can read more about Partnerships as a form of business legal structure in section 3.6.1.)

You as an Investor

Never forget that you might be your own best source of funding. One nice thing about using your own money is that you aren't obligated to anyone else or any other organization—it is yours to invest. This can be an excellent solution for individuals with some credit problems.

To raise your own capital, you can:

- Cash out stocks, bonds, life insurance, an IRA, RRSP, or other retirement account
- Increase your credit on charge cards (remember that you will pay high interest rates on these)
- Use personal savings
- Take out a second mortgage or home equity loan on your house or other property
- Sell something valuable, like a car, jewelry, real estate, or art

3.5.5 Government Programs

Small Business Administration Loans

The Small Business Administration (SBA) doesn't actually lend you money. However, they have a program called the "7(a) Loan Program" in which they work with banks to provide loan services to small business owners. The SBA guarantees a percentage of the loan that a commercial lender will give you, so that if you default on your payments, the bank will still get back the amount guaranteed by the SBA. Both the bank and the SBA share the risk in lending money to you. As the borrower, you are still responsible for the full amount of the loan.

When you apply for a small business loan, you will actually apply at your local bank. The bank then decides whether they will make the loan internally or use the SBA program. Under this program, the government does not provide any financial contribution, and does not make loans itself.

The SBA also provides a pre-qualification program that assists business start-ups in putting together a viable funding request package for submission to lenders. They will work with you to help you apply for a loan up to a maximum amount of $250,000. Once the loan package has been submitted, studied, and approved by the SBA, they will issue a commitment letter on your behalf that you can submit to lenders for consideration.

In essence, the SBA gives lenders the reassurance that they will pay back the loan if you don't. They provide the extra assurance that many lenders need to get entrepreneurs the financing they need. You can read more about the process at **www.sba.gov** (click on "Services" then on "Financial Assistance").

The SBA also has a "Micro-Loans" program, which offers loans to start-up and newly established businesses through non-profit entities at the local level up to a maximum of $35,000. The average loan is about $13,000. Interest rates for these small loans vary between about 8 to 13 percent. You can find out more about these loans at the SBA website.

Government Programs in Canada

If you are planning to open a retail business in Canada, you might be interested in the Business Development Bank of Canada (BDC) or the Canada Small Business Financing Program (CSBF). The BDC is a financial institution owned by the federal government that offers consulting and financing services to help get small businesses started. They also have a financing program aimed specifically at women entrepreneurs. You can learn more about the Business Development Bank of Canada (BDC) and its financing resources at **www.bdc.ca**.

The Canada Small Business Financing Program is much like the SBA 7(a) Loan Program mentioned earlier in this section. The maximum amount you can borrow is $250,000, and the funds must be used to purchase real property, leasehold improvements or equipment. The CSBFP works with lenders across the country to offer loans at 3% above the lender's prime lending rate. To find out more, visit **www.ic.gc.ca/eic/site/csbfp-pfpec.nsf/eng/h_la02855.html**.

3.6 Legal Matters

3.6.1 Your Business Legal Structure

Your business structure affects the cost of starting your business, your taxes, and your responsibility for any debts the business incurs. This section will highlight the several different legal forms a business can have. There are four basic structures: sole proprietorship, partnership, corporation (including the S corporation), and limited liability company (LLC).

Sole Proprietorship

If you want to run the business yourself, without incorporating, your business will be known as a "sole proprietorship." This is the least expensive way to start a business. It is also the easiest because it requires less paperwork and you can report your business income on your personal tax return. All you need to do is apply for an occupational business license in the area where your business will be located. Usually, the license doesn't take long to be processed and you can begin operations fairly quickly.

If you're running the business by yourself, your social security number can serve as your tax-payer identification number. If you have employees, you'll need to request a taxpayer identification number from the Internal Revenue Service.

A sole proprietorship means that you have almost total control of the business and all the profits. The only drawback to this type of business is that you are personally liable for any debts of the business.

Advantages

- Easy to start
- Low start-up costs
- Flexible and informal
- Business losses can often be deducted from personal income for tax purposes

Disadvantages

- Unlimited personal liability: the sole proprietor can be held personally responsible for debts and judgments placed against the business. This means that all personal income and assets, not just those of the business, can be seized to recoup losses or pay damages.
- All business income earned must be reported and is taxed as personal income.
- More difficult to raise capital for the business

Sole proprietorships are extremely common and popular among small business owners — mostly because they are easy and cheap to start with the least amount of paperwork.

Partnership

If you want to go into business with someone else, the easiest and least expensive way to do this is by forming a partnership. Legally, you would both be responsible for any debts of the company and you would enter into something called a partnership agreement. There are two types of partnerships: general partnerships and limited partnerships.

A general partnership is when two or more people get together and start a business. They agree on the conduction of the business and how the profits, risks, liabilities and losses will be distributed between them.

TIP: Partnerships don't have to be divided equally between all partners. However, all partners must agree on how the profit, risk, liability and loss will be divided.

A limited partnership is when one or more partners invest in the business, but are not involved in the everyday operations. Limited partners are investors — partners — but they have limited say in the hands-on operations.

Partnerships usually have more financial clout than sole proprietorships — a definite advantage — simply because they have more in the way of assets than a single person. Another advantage to a partnership is, in an ideal situation, you and your partner will balance out each other's strengths and weaknesses. On the other hand, many businesses have gone bad because of an ill fitted partnership.

Below are some of the advantages and disadvantages to partnerships:

Advantages

- More initial equity for start-up costs
- Broader areas of expertise can lead to increased opportunities
- Lower start-up costs than incorporation
- Some tax advantages

Disadvantages

- All partners are equally liable for the other's mistakes with the same liability as a sole proprietorship
- Profits and losses must be shared
- The business must be dissolved and reorganized when a partner leaves

Working with a Partner

Beyond any legal issues, before going into business with a partner you should spend many hours talking about how you will work together, including:

- What each of you will be responsible for.
- How you will make decisions on a day-to-day basis.
- What percentage of the business each of you will own.
- How you see the business developing in the future.
- What you expect from each other.

During your discussions you can learn if there are any areas where you need to compromise. You can avoid future misunderstandings by putting the points you have agreed on into your written partnership agreement that covers any possibility you can think of (including if one of you leave the business in the future).

Corporation

Whether you are working alone or with partners, if you want a more formal legal structure for your business, you can incorporate. Incorporation can protect you from personal liability and may make your business appear more professional.

However, it usually costs several hundred dollars and there are many rules and regulations involved with this type of business structure (among other requirements, corporations must file articles of incorporation, hold regular meetings, and keep records of those meetings). Many new business owners consult with an attorney before incorporating.

Here is a list of some of the advantages and disadvantages to incorporating your business.

Advantages

- Protect personal assets and income from liability by separating your business income and assets from your personal.
- Corporations get greater tax breaks and incentives
- Ownership can be sold or transferred if the owner wishes to retire or leave the business
- Banks and other lending institutions tend to have more faith in incorporated businesses so raising capital is easier

Disadvantages

- Increased start-up costs
- Substantial increase in paperwork
- Your business losses cannot be offset against your personal income
- Corporations are more closely regulated

S Corporation

The IRS offers a provision, called an S corporation, where a corporation can be taxed as a sole proprietorship. An S Corporation is similar to the corporation in most ways, but with some tax advantages. The corporation can pass its earnings and profits on as dividends to the shareholder(s). However, as an employee of the corporation you do have to pay yourself a wage that meets the government's reasonable standards of compensation just as if you were paying someone else to do your job.

Unless you want to wind up paying both a personal income tax and a business tax, you will probably want to create an S corporation. This saves you money because you are taxed at an individual rate instead of a corporate rate.

Limited Liability Company

A Limited Liability Company, or LLC, is a relatively new type of business legal structure in the U.S. It is a combination of a partnership and a corporation, and is considered to have some of the best attributes of both, including limited personal liability.

A limited liability company is legally separate from the person or persons who own it and offers some protections that a partnership does not. Partners in a limited liability company get the same personal financial protection as those in a corporation.

The LLC business structure gives you the benefits of a partnership or S corporation while providing personal asset protection like a corporation. Similar to incorporating, there will be substantial paperwork involved in establishing this business structure. LLCs have flexible tax options, but are usually taxed like a partnership.

Here are some of the advantages and disadvantages of LLCs:

Advantages

- Limited liability similar to a corporation
- Tax advantages similar to a corporation
- Can be started with one (except in Massachusetts) or more members like a sole proprietorship or partnership

Disadvantages

- More costly to start than a sole proprietorship or partnership
- Consensus among members may become an issue
- LLC dissolves if any member leaves

Regulations regarding limited liability companies vary from area to area. Make sure you do your homework if this interests you.

In the end, choosing a business legal structure for your company is a personal choice, and the advantages and disadvantages should be considered thoroughly. Many small business owners begin their independent venture as a sole proprietorship because of the low costs, and incorporate as the business grows and becomes larger and more complex.

For more on business structures take a look at the resources available at FindLaw.com (**http://smallbusiness.findlaw.com/business-structures**). For some additional government resources to help you decide which structure to choose, try the SBA Small Business Planner at **www.sba.gov/smallbusinessplanner**. In the "Start Your Business" section, open the "Choose a Structure" link. In Canada, you can find more information about business structures at the Canada Business Services for Entrepreneurs website (**www.canadabusiness.ca/eng/125/141**).

3.6.2 Business Licenses

Regardless of what form of legal structure you choose for your business, you'll need to obtain business licenses. This is not a difficult task. All it normally entails is filling out some forms and paying an annual license fee. Contact your city or county clerk's office for more information about registering your business. Contact information can be found in your phone book or online through resources such as Business.gov at **www.business.gov/register/licenses-and-permits**.

There may also be a number of other permits and licenses you will need:

- EIN (Employer Identification Number) from the IRS or a BN (Business Number) in Canada. All businesses that have employees need a federal identification number with which to report employee tax withholding information.

- Retail businesses that collect sales tax must be registered with their state's Department of Revenue and get a state identification number. In Canada, you will need to register to collect the Goods and Services Tax (GST), as well as provincial sales tax (except in Alberta), or Harmonized Sales Tax (the HST blends provincial sales tax and GST together in one tax).
- If you are putting up a new building for your store, you will need to ensure you have appropriate permits and comply with any requirements for zoning or access for people with disabilities (see section 4.1.2).

Food permits are required for restaurants and other food-serving establishments in the United States. To find out what permits are required for your store, check with the health departments of your state, county, and municipality.

Links to all of the states' departments of public health are available at **www.foodsafety.gov/about/state/index.html**. (Look for the "Find My State Agency" map and drop-down menu). A list of provincial health authorities is available at **www.inspection.gc.ca/english/fssa/concen/restaure.shtml**. Search within the Health and Sanitation section of the state or municipal code rather than the Business Regulations and Licenses section.

Municipalities generally require permits and licenses or charge fees for other food-establishment issues, such as food consumed on premise and food consumed off premise, ice cream carts (such as those used for special events), special events signs, and health inspection fees. To find out what business regulations and licenses are required for your municipality, city, or town, check its municipal code online. Most cities and towns post their bylaws on their websites.

For information about local, state, and federal requirements in the U.S. visit the SBA Small Business Planner (**www.sba.gov/smallbusiness planner**) and choose "Get Licenses and Permits" in the "Start Your Business" section. In Canada, business licenses and health permits are issued at the municipal level so check with your local municipality for help with acquiring a business license. For a province-by-province list of Canadian municipalities and their websites, visit the BizPal website at **www.bizpal.**

ca/part_partners.shtml. Many municipalities offer business license applications right on their websites.

3.6.3 Taxes

If you are properly informed and prepared you won't have to face your tax responsibility with a feeling of dread. In fact, once you are organized and you have enlisted the help of a good tax professional, taxes become just another regular business task.

Get Informed First

The best thing you can do to be sure of your personal and business tax obligations is to find the information you need before you start your new store. The Internal Revenue Service (IRS) has a number of informative documents online that you can look at today to learn the basics about everything you need to prepare for your taxes as a small business owner. If you read these documents and understand them, you will have no surprises at tax time.

One helpful document is the Tax Guide for Small Businesses that outlines your rights and responsibilities as a small business owner. It tells you how to file your taxes, and provides an overview of the tax system for small businesses. You can find this document at **www.irs.gov/pub/irs-pdf/p334.pdf**. For more general information for small business owners from the IRS visit their website at **www.irs.gov/businesses/small/index.html**.

For Canadian residents, the Canada Revenue Agency also provides basic tax information for new business owners. This includes information about the GST, how to file your taxes, allowable expenses and so on. You can find this information and more helpful documents at **www.cra-arc.gc.ca/tx/bsnss/menu-eng.html**.

It is also important to be informed about your tax obligations on a state and local level. Tax laws and requirements vary on a state-by-state basis and locally, too. Make sure that you find out exactly what you are responsible for in your state and city. In addition, it is important to find out about sales tax in your area.

The Federation of Tax Administrators website provides information on a state-by-state basis for personal, sales and other taxes. Visit **www.taxadmin.org/fta/link**, where you will find a clickable map of the United States. Look for a "Businesses" or "Small Business" link on your state's revenue agency website and then a "Sales or Other Use Taxes" link (or something similar). The Canada Revenue Agency has a linked directory of government websites at **www.cra-arc.gc.ca/tx/bsnss/prv_lnks-eng.html** where you can find tax information on a province-by-province basis.

Getting Assistance

If you decide you would prefer a qualified tax professional to help you handle your taxes, you will find you are in good company. Many small business owners decide to have a professional handle their taxes. An accountant can point out deductions you might otherwise miss and save you a lot of money.

One resource that may assist you in choosing an accountant is the article "Finding an Accountant" by Kevin McDonald. It offers helpful advice for finding an accounting professional whose expertise matches your needs. The article is available at **www.bankrate.com/brm/news/advice/19990609c.asp**.

Once you've determined what your accounting needs are you may be able to find a professional accountant at the Accountant Finder website (**www.accountant-finder.com**). This site offers a clickable map of the United States with links to accountants in cities across the country. Alternatively, the Yellow Pages directory for your city is a good place to find listings for accountants.

You will also need to understand payroll taxes if you plan on hiring employees. Each new employee needs to fill out paperwork prior to their first pay check being issued. In the U.S. this will be a W-4 and an I-9 form. In Canada, the employee will have to complete a T-4 and fill out a Canada Pension form. Both the W-4 and the T-4 are legal documents verifying the tax deductions a new employee has. The amount of tax you will withhold as an employer varies and is based on the required deductions an employee has as specified by the federal government. Make sure you retain the forms in a folder labeled with their name and store them in a readily accessible place such as a filing cabinet in your office.

Check with your state or province's labor office to make sure you are clear about all the forms employees must fill out in order to work for you. The sites below give more information on legal paperwork, including where to get blank copies of the forms your employees will need to fill out.

- *SmartLegalForms.com*
  (Sells employee forms online)
  www.hrlawinfo.com/index.asp

- *GovDocs Employee Records and Personnel Forms*
  (Click on "Employee Records")
  www.hrdocs.com/Posters/hrproducts

- *Canada Revenue Agency*
  (Download and print any form you need)
  www.cra-arc.gc.ca/forms/

3.6.4 Insurance

Insurance can help protect the investment you make in your company from unforeseen circumstances or disaster.

Types of insurance for a retail business include:

Property Insurance

Property insurance protects the contents of your business (e.g. your computer, your merchandise, etc.) in case of fire, theft, or other losses. If you lease space, you may need property insurance only on your own merchandise and equipment if the owner of the building has insurance on the property.

Liability Insurance

This insurance (also known as Errors and Omissions Insurance) protects you against loss if you are sued for alleged negligence. It could pay judgments against you (up to the policy limits) along with any legal fees you incur defending yourself — for example, if a customer has an adverse reaction to your ice cream or one of your frozen desserts and becomes sick and then decides to sue you and your company.

> **TIP:** For some small businesses, getting a Business Owner's policy is a good place to start. These policies are designed for small business owners with under one hundred employees and revenue of under one million dollars. These policies combine liability and property insurance together. Small business owners like these policies because of their convenience and affordable premiums. You can find out more about these policies at the Insurance Information Institute (**www.iii.org/insurance_topics**).

Car Insurance

Be sure to ask your broker about your auto insurance if you'll be using your personal vehicle on company business.

Business Interruption Insurance

This insurance covers your bills while you are out of operation for a covered loss, such as a fire. This type of insurance covers ongoing expenses such as rent or taxes until your business is running again.

Life and Disability Insurance

If you provide a portion of your family's income, consider life insurance and disability insurance to make certain they are cared for if something happens to you. If you become sick or otherwise disabled for an extended period, your business could be in jeopardy. Disability insurance would provide at least a portion of your income while you're not able to be working.

Health Insurance

If you live in the United States and aren't covered under a spouse's health plan, you'll need to consider your health insurance options. You can compare health insurance quotes at **www.ehealthinsurance.com**, which offers plans from over 150 insurance companies nationwide.

Canadians have most of their health care expenses covered by the Canadian government. For expenses that are not covered (such as dental care, eyeglasses, prescription drugs, etc.) self-employed professionals may get tax benefits from setting up their own private health care plan. Puhl Employee Benefits (**www.puhlemployeebenefits.com**) is an example of the type of financial planning company that can help you set up your own private health care plan.

Association Member Policies

Some insurance companies offer discount pricing for members of particular organizations. When you are looking for organizations to join, whether your local Chamber of Commerce or a national association, check to see if discounted health insurance is one of the member benefits.

The following associations offer or plan to offer insurance plans to their members:

- *National Ice Cream Retailers Association (NICRA)*
  At the time of publication, NICRA was in the process of obtaining quotes for group health and life insurance, disability, dental, vision, liability, and workers compensation.
  www.nicra.org/benefits.html

- *Great Lakes Ice Cream & Fast Food Association (GLICFFA)*
  This association offers health insurance as part of a group insurance package to qualified members. The package includes building, liability, and workers compensation in addition to health insurance. Full details available to members only.
  www.glicffa.com/index.aspx?aspxerrorpath=/Membership.aspx

- *National Restaurant Association (NRA)*
  Many of the state restaurant associations of the NRA offer members discounts on health insurance. Coverage, benefits, and costs vary by each participating state. To find out whether your state's restaurant association provides health insurance benefits, check its website. You can locate the website of each state's restaurant association through the clickable map at:
  www.restaurant.org/states/index.cfm

Workers' Compensation Insurance

Another type of insurance to consider if you plan to hire employees is workers' compensation insurance. Most states in the U.S. and provinces in Canada require businesses to have workers' compensation insurance to help protect their employees in case of injury on the job.

To find what workers' compensation laws govern your business in your state check out the Southern Association of Workers' Compensation Administrators' site (**www.sawca.com/workerscomplinks.htm**). It has links to the various states' workers' compensation sites. In Canada you should visit the Association of Workers' Compensation Boards of Canada website where you can find information about the WCB for your province. Visit them at **www.awcbc.org**.

More Information

There are other types of insurance and different levels of coverage available for each type. An insurance broker (check the Yellow Pages) can advise you of your options and shop around for the best rates for you. You might want to check out the SBA's in-depth risk management guide that covers most aspects of insurance planning for small business. You can read it on their website at **www.sba.gov/tools/resourcelibrary/publications/index.html** (click on "Management and Planning Series", then scroll down to #17).

3.6.5 Other Regulations

Food Service

All food establishments in Canada and the United States are required to comply with regulations governing food service. These laws govern how food is stored, handled, displayed, served, and even defined. They also govern the physical environment and sanitary conditions of any facility serving food.

As an owner of an ice cream shop, you will be responsible for such things as:

- Maintaining the required freezer temperatures
- Using specific types of freezer/product thermometers

- Sanitizing all work surfaces
- Ensuring food servers handle food properly
- Protecting food on display from potential customer contamination
- Disposing of waste properly
- Providing warm water, soap, and individual paper towels for employee hand washing
- Storing first-aid supplies away from possible food contamination
- Ventilating all rooms so they are free of excessive heat, obnoxious odors, and condensation
- Providing permanent light fixtures that meet minimum light tolerances over food preparation areas

Check your state or province's administrative code for detailed information on the requirements governing your operations.

Food Safety and Health Inspections

All food establishments in Canada and the United States are required to follow all applicable sanitation, food safety, and health regulations. Establishments serving food are regularly inspected by the governing health authority or agency to ensure they are meeting these standards. Typical areas that are inspected in an ice cream shop include how food is stored and handled, freezer temperatures, water temperatures, restrooms, lighting, employee hygiene practices, signs of insect or rodent infestation, and overall cleanliness.

Check your state's website for information on food codes and inspections (see section 3.6.2), or check the state and municipal codes for all regulations governing health and sanitation in an ice cream shop. (See section 3.6.2 for ways to locate this information.)

Smoking Regulations

Many cities, counties, and states restrict or forbid smoking in food establishments and near building entrances. For example, some states and municipalities forbid smoking inside any food establishment. Others also prohibit any smoking within a specified number of feet from the building and its entrances. And still other cities and towns forbid any outdoor smoking. Check with your local health department to identify any smoking restrictions both inside and outside your shop.

Menu Regulations

Many states require that food establishments provide nutritional information for all standard items on the menu, such as calories. Restaurants with fewer than 10 locations nationwide are exempt from this requirement, but laws vary from state to state. Check with your state's Department of Public Health to verify if your menu or display board must contain this information.

Government Regulations for Commercial Ice Cream Production

If you will be producing ice cream on a commercial basis, you will also need to adhere to government regulations governing this activity. You'll need to pay strict attention to the definitions in the legislation that apply to your products. In particular, the milk or butter fat content of ice cream and other frozen desserts is strictly defined for each type of product. If you plan to offer organic products, the National Organic Program in the U.S. governs the use of terms like "certified organic" and there are penalties for noncompliance. To read more about these regulations, visit the websites below.

- *U.S. Department of Agriculture Standards for Commercial Ice Cream*
  www.ams.usda.gov/AMSv1.0/getfile?dDocName=STELDEV3004477

- *Canada Food and Drug Act Ice Cream Regulations*
  (See page 302 of the document)
  http://laws.justice.gc.ca/PDF/Regulation/C/C.R.C.,_c._870.pdf

- *Organic Ice Cream: USDA National Organic Program*
  (Click on "I Want To: Find an AMS Program" then scroll down to "National Organic Program". On the next page, click on "I Want To: Get Certified")
  www.ams.usda.gov

4. Setting Up Your Ice Cream Shop

Your business plan is written, you have your financing, the legal issues have been dealt with, and all the licenses are in place. You're ready to set up your store. In this chapter, we'll look at the various aspects of putting it all together, from finding a location through how to finish off the interior of your store, to the equipment, supplies and inventory you will need.

4.1 Finding a Location

You have probably heard it before and it's true: location can make or break your store. Finding a space that suits you can take a little work, but once you have the perfect location, the thrill of opening your own retail store will be that much closer! While location can mean the difference between success and failure, you also have to consider your budget. How much rent can you afford? Prime locations often have a prime price tag on them as well. You may have to start smaller and work your way up to the store you can afford.

4.1.1 Possible Locations

Storefronts and Stand-alone Buildings

Retail space can be found in numerous locations throughout any community. Options for ice cream shops include storefronts and stand alone buildings near residential areas, business districts or downtown areas, and near popular tourist areas. An important factor to consider when choosing a location is its proximity to your target market. If you are targeting young customers with ample disposable income, a site across from a high school or college may be the ideal location. The same site might not be the best choice for a cozy shop targeting high-income customers or theatergoers looking for a late-night dessert. Factors to consider include the following: How far is the location from places where your potential customers live, shop, work, and frequent? What attractions are nearby? What kind of foot traffic is there in the area? Does activity in the area slow during certain times or days of the week? How far is the nearest competitor? What type of store was in this location before?

Sites that have heavy foot traffic and/or are easily accessible by car often make the best location. Many ice cream shops do well near train stations, retail stores, other restaurants, sports facilities, theaters, in downtown areas, and in shopping malls. Parking is an important consideration. Is ample parking provided? Is it easy to get in and out of the parking lot? Is it on a heavily traveled or high-speed road? A shop at a busy intersection that experiences frequent traffic jams or bottlenecks may be less desirable than one in a less-dense area with easy access to a parking lot.

Another important feature is visibility. A shop tucked in a courtyard or off the beaten path may have all the features you want, but if your potential customers have difficulty finding it or don't even know it exists, it is not the best location. Visibility is key. The best locations are those that are highly visible, easily accessible, and near other sites that attract traffic.

Malls

Shopping malls and strip malls are good options for shops that target impulse buyers. Visibility, high foot traffic, and nearby competition are important features to consider when searching locations in a shopping mall. Traffic patterns, accessibility, and parking are factors to consider for strip malls. Questions to ask about potential mall locations include the following: Who are the mall's clientele? What are their in-mall food spending habits? What other stores and restaurants are nearby? What other ice cream shops are in the mall? Is the location near a mall entrance or meeting spot? How visible is this location?

Stores on main corridors of shopping malls have greater visibility than shops on side wings, but they also have higher rents. Proximity to other food establishments can be both an advantage and disadvantage. Many shoppers head for areas with a high concentration of shops serving food and then browse for the one that meets their requirements. Mall shops often target families with children, so a location near stores frequented by these shoppers, such as toy stores, children's stores, and specialty stores, may be advantageous.

An important consideration for a strip mall location is the other tenants. What retail stores are in the strip mall and who frequents these shops? Stores that attract customers similar to your target market can help to attract customers to your shop.

When considering a location, check to ensure that it is easily visible. Imagine your shop in the location and ask yourself, "Will shoppers hurrying past notice my shop? Will it grab their attention?"

Outdoor Malls/Mall Kiosks

Many malls offer small booths for lease on a short-term basis (you've probably seen them spring up around the holidays to take advantage of the extra consumer purchases during that time of year). However, they can be expensive, depending upon the mall. Smaller privately owned malls will sometimes offer a lower rent for a percentage of your profits. Larger malls are less likely to offer such incentives as they have an easier time leasing the space.

Mall kiosks also can be located in food courts in malls. These locations usually are in high traffic corridors and may have high rents. Mall kiosks can also be located in outdoor malls or unique locations (see the next section).

Unique Locations

Depending on your target market, you may want to consider setting up shop within a train station, amusement or theme park, convention center, hotel, college or university, casino, along a waterfront or on a pier, or in a hotel or resort. These settings provide high-profile visibility and ready access to a select market segment. Disadvantages include the possibility of very high rent and high competition from other food vendors. If your shop is targeting a specific group, one of these locations may be the best site.

> *"The most important piece of advice I could give to someone considering owning an ice cream shop would be — Location, Location, Location! Do your homework on the location."*
>
> — Pam Nardinelli, owner, Marble Slab Creamery

4.1.2 Points to Consider

You probably have some idea about where you envision your store's location and what sort of a space you are looking for. But to make sure that you don't get stuck with something you are unhappy with, be as definite as possible about all the particulars you are looking for in a space before you begin your search. As you begin to consider what you need in a space, think about three things:

- Things you must have
- Things you would like to have but can live without
- Things that you definitely want to avoid

Very likely, the first "must have" will be a particular amount of space.

How Much Space Do You Need?

Ice cream retail shops can range in size from 100 square feet to 4,000 square feet or more. Around 1,000 to 1,200 square feet of floor space is adequate for many ice cream retail operations. This gives you enough room to have sufficient space for product display and service counters, as well as room for customers to queue for service and eat their selections on site. Stores offering table service will need more space, and those with none or very limited seating can operate with less space.

However, many new business ice cream shop owners occasionally start out in much smaller spaces such as 600-800 square feet and expand or relocate once their businesses have become successful. Anything smaller than this and your store will start to feel too cramped for your customers' comfort.

If you have too little space, customers may feel uncomfortable waiting. Giving ample room for customers to browse product selections helps customers to identify what they want to order before they arrive at the service counter and keeps the line moving smoothly and prevents bottlenecks.

Space is often costly, though, because many retail property owners charge rent by the square foot. You may wind up having to compromise and, if you do, it can be important to limit your inventory accordingly so you do not "overstuff" your store. (Tips on using space are covered in section 4.2.)

Legal Requirements

Another vital issue is ensuring the space meets all the legal requirements for running your store. Consider the following issues as you begin your search for your new store location.

Permits and Zoning

If you are going to make improvements to your space, you will need to make sure that you check your local city, county, and state regulations and get the proper permits to proceed.

Another thing to ask your potential landlord or your local government's zoning department is whether or not the space you are considering renting is zoned as a retail space.

The difference between zoning and the need for a permit is relatively simple. Zoning indicates where a business is allowed by local law to be set up, while permits designate whether a business can operate or not. (For example, many municipalities allow retail pet shops in areas that are zoned for retail, but one selling prohibited exotic species would never get a permit to operate.)

Many jurisdictions also require new business owners to obtain a Certificate of Occupancy. The requirements vary from area to area but many cities require inspections before issuing the certificate.

Access for People with Disabilities

As part of the Americans with Disabilities Act (you can read about the requirements of this legislation at **www.usdoj.gov/crt/ada/adahom1.htm**), businesses are required to provide access for people with disabilities. Similar laws exist in Canada (check with your local municipality). Accessibility requirements may include:

- Floor aisles wide enough for wheelchairs
- Wheelchair ramps
- Wheelchair elevators if steps are present
- Rails in handicapped restrooms

Make sure to discuss this with any landlord you are considering renting space from.

Other Points to Consider

Here are some additional questions to ask:

- In what part of town would I like to locate my store?
- Are any nearby stores similar enough to my store to be direct competition?
- Are any national chain restaurants or ice cream franchisors, that would affect my business close to the area where I would like to locate my store?
- Are there other businesses or services nearby that might attract customer traffic to my store, such as movie theaters, bookstores, sports centers, or bowling alleys?
- Have I observed car traffic near my store at different times of the day?
- How much foot traffic does this location get?

In addition to these questions, you should consider the following points when looking for your retail space:

- *Parking:* Make sure the parking is close enough to your shop for customers to make it convenient to get to your shop without walking far. If they need to pay for the parking, can you offer a validation service?
- *Price:* Sure that spot on Main Street is ideal, but how much will you have to sell in order to afford it? Don't put yourself in financial distress right out of the starting gate; be realistic.
- *Projecting costs:* Calculate how much this space will actually cost. Ask about utilities, taxes, any extra fees you might have to pay.

Considering all these issues should help you narrow down the list of places to consider. The checklist below has a longer list of questions to help you assess the places you decide to check out.

Keeping Track of Places You've Seen

As you look at properties for the perfect potential space for your new store, keep track of where you have been, what each potential space looked like, and the positives and negatives of each space.

Consider taking along a digital camera on your space-hunting trips to take a picture of each space's exterior and interior so you can more easily remember details of each location later.

To make the process easier, use the checklist provided below for each of your space hunting excursions. This checklist, along with a picture or two, will help you to be really clear about each potential location you visit so you can make an informed decision.

4.1.3 Signing Your Lease

Signing a lease for your store space is quite a bit more than putting your signature at the bottom of a legal document. There are a variety of different lease options you can have and a number of things to consider when putting together the details in your lease.

Finding Your Perfect Space Checklist

Date: ________________ **Location:** ____________________________

Pictures

- ❑ Exterior front
- ❑ Interior
- ❑ Notes on pictures

Space Location Checklist

- ❑ Does the space have easy freeway access? Which ones?
- ❑ Does the space have handy public transportation? Where and what?
- ❑ Is the quality of the neighborhood good?
- ❑ What possibly helpful businesses are nearby?
- ❑ What possibly detrimental businesses are nearby?

Exterior Checklist

- ❑ How is the overall appearance of the building exterior? Does it need any obvious work? What?
- ❑ Is the building a storefront location?
- ❑ Is there a garden or parking strip area? Who maintains it?
- ❑ Where is the trash area? Is trash pick up included as part of the lease agreement?
- ❑ Is the tenant responsible for sidewalk maintenance? Shoveling snow? General clean up of trash and debris?

Interior Checklist

- ❑ How is the overall appearance of the building interior? Does it need any obvious work? What?
- ❑ What is the square footage of the space? Is there any room to grow?
- ❑ Are the windows functional? Are there enough windows?
- ❑ Is there adequate light?
- ❑ Are the air conditioning and heating systems shared or private for each tenant?
- ❑ Is the ventilation system shared or private for each tenant?
- ❑ Is the space technology-ready?
- ❑ Will you be able to use your own already existing Internet Service Provider if you have one?
- ❑ Is the space wired for cable modem or DSL?
- ❑ Is the space wired for phone lines? How many?
- ❑ Does the space have private or shared restroom facilities? What is the overall state of the existing restroom facilities? Are they wheelchair accessible?
- ❑ Does the space have hot and cold running water?
- ❑ Are there existing janitorial services and is the cost for this service part of the lease price?
- ❑ Does the space have a workroom or break room?
- ❑ Does the space have a kitchen?

Extra Charges

- ❑ What services and utilities are included in the lease price?
- ❑ What services and utilities are provided by the landlord for a fee?
- ❑ What services and utilities are the responsibility of the tenant?

Shared Tenant Services, Spaces, Costs, Responsibilities

- ❑ Are there any shared tenant spaces?
- ❑ Are there any shared tenant responsibilities?
- ❑ Is there a mandatory tenant association?
- ❑ Are there any costs that tenants are required to share?

Extra Benefits and Features

- ❑ Are there any extra benefits or features that make this space especially desirable?

Notes:

Be sure the following things are clearly stated:

- Who is responsible for what repairs?
- What types of signs can you use? Are there any restrictions on sidewalk sales or signs to draw customers into the store?
- Can you change the colors and décor of the store? (Some malls have very specific rules.)
- Can you make alterations to suit your needs?
- Is there any security?

What to Include in a Lease

Your lease is the legal agreement that makes it clear what each party will do (or won't do). Therefore it is vital that you get everything you expect regarding your store space written into the lease. For example, once you have located a space you really like there still may be a number of improvements that you want to have happen before you move in.

Regular Improvements

Regular improvements are the things that a landlord will do for any prospective tenant — no matter what their business. These are the things that need to be done to prepare the space. Some of the things you should expect (although you should check just to be sure) include:

- Having the space prepared and cleaned by a professional janitorial service
- Painting the interior or exterior of the building as part of normal wear and tear
- Replacing worn bathroom fixtures, mini blinds, or broken fixtures
- Replacing worn or damaged carpet or flooring

Specific Improvements Requests

Specific improvements are the things you want to see done to your space to make it the way you dream it should be. This might include:

- Adding partitions
- Installing a door or a window

- Creating storage or office space
- A break room for employees

In short, these improvements are the things you might hire a contractor to do.

Based on the term of your lease (a longer-term lease makes a landlord more willing to help fund improvements), your landlord will need to agree to the specific improvements that you want to make to the space and all of this will need to be included in the lease agreement. You must determine what the landlord will let you do, what the landlord will fund, what you will need to fund, and who will do the work.

> **TIP:** If the space you are considering needs too many improvements, maybe you haven't found the right space. Consider looking for a space that fits more of your needs before you commit to a long or complicated improvement plan.

Types of Leases

First you will need to consider the type of lease that will work best for your store. Your lease will most likely fall into one of these categories:

Month-to-Month Lease

A month-to-month lease is the most flexible kind of lease agreement you can have. If you think you might want to get out of your lease quickly, all that is necessary to do so is 30 days notice. Naturally, there is a downside to this sort of a lease. With a month-to-month lease, you aren't locked into a price for a reasonable length of time, plus the landlord can ask you to leave with 30 days notice.

Short-Term Fixed Rate Lease

While a short-term fixed rate lease has all the benefits of a shorter month-to-month lease, it also locks you into a fixed price for the length of the lease. This sort of commitment might be wise if you are truly concerned about giving up your current job to open your store and want a short amount of time to see if it will really work. With a short-term lease, you can add verbiage in the lease to determine what happens after the lease ends. What happens next is up to you and the landlord to negotiate.

Long-Term Lease

A long-term lease is a lease with a term of a year or more. Long-term leases that are for several years or even longer are called "multi-year leases." The best thing about a long-term lease is that once you find a great space, you can stay there for as long as you want.

Negotiating Leases

Be very careful when negotiating a lease. If you commit to paying $1,200 a month for two years, that is nearly $30,000. Try to get the shortest term lease available, especially as you start out. There is a possibility this could backfire and you could lose your space, but finding a new space is a better alternative than owing thousands of dollars on a store that is not thriving.

Some store owners don't realize that a lease document prepared and presented by a potential landlord is a negotiating tool. You certainly don't have to accept the terms of a lease that you are uncomfortable with, and you can negotiate for the things you would like to see either added to or removed from the lease.

The lease written by a landlord is written in the landlord's best interests, not yours, so look for what you feel needs to be changed or amended to make the lease fit your requirements. Remember, the process of signing a lease is a negotiating experience. Both you and your landlord will probably need to bend a little to come up with a document that works well for both of you.

Don't feel pressured into signing a lease as soon as it is handed to you. Plan on taking the document away with you so you can read it carefully, and, if you wish, show it to a qualified attorney for advice. Good advice on leasing, including an article on "Negotiating the Best Commercial Lease Terms" can be found at **www.nolo.com/legal-encyclopedia/business-licenses/index.html** (scroll down to the "Your Business Space and Commercial Lease" section).

Sample Lease with Comments

In the sample lease below, we will point out potential problem areas. Note that the comments are simply suggestions about some matters you may want to consider. These are opinions based on our research, and do not come from a lawyer or a commercial real estate agent. As your own situation is unique, make sure you have a lawyer who is familiar with business leases look over any lease before you sign it.

Opening Section

This lease is made between Big Commercial Landlord, herein after called the Lessor, and Ima Yogurtseller, hereinafter called the Lessee.

This is a pretty standard clause in any contract and simply states who are the parties to the lease agreement. If you are a corporation, then you may want to try to use your corporate name as the Lessee. Sometimes, this clause will include your home address.

Lessee herby offers to lease from Lessor the premises located in the city of Greenfield, in the County of Hancock, in the State of Indiana, described as 197 State Street, Suite C, based upon the terms and conditions as outlined below.

This clause outlines the specific space you are agreeing to lease. Things to watch for would be any mistakes in the address. If it is a building with several store spaces, double check that the suite number is correct. You could wind up leasing more square feet than you wanted or losing a prime location.

1. Term and Rent

Lessee agrees to rent the above premises for a term of two years, commencing September 1, 2008, and terminating on August 31, 2010, or sooner as provided herein at the annual rental of 7,200 dollars ($7,200.00), payable in equal monthly installments of 600 dollars ($600.00) in advance on the first day of each month for that month's rental, during the term of this lease. All payments should be made directly to the Lessor at the address specified in paragraph one.

Some of this information is a little hard to break down, but section 1 basically outlines how much rent you will be paying. Double check that the monthly rent matches the yearly sum. Be sure the day you have agreed to is the day that the rent is due and not sooner. Also, you might want to try to get a shorter term on the lease, if possible. Many landlords will negotiate on this point. Two years is standard.

2. Use

Lessee shall use and occupy the premises for an art gallery operation called YoDazzle. The location shall be used for no other purpose. Lessor represents that the premises may lawfully be used for the purpose stated above.

This simply states what your business will be. The thing to be most cautious of here is making sure that all things are listed. One thing that jumps right out in the above description is that it does not allow for retail sales of other items besides the main retail sector merchandise. You may want to add additional complementary lines of merchandise that aren't directly related to the main retail business you're in. You should ask to have this added before signing the lease.

3. Care and Maintenance of the Premises

Lessee recognizes that the premises are in good repair, unless otherwise indicated herein. Lessee shall, at the Lessee's own expense and at all times, maintain the premises in good and safe order, including plate glass, electrical wiring, plumbing and heating and any other equipment on the premises. Lessee shall return the same at termination of contract, in as good condition as received, normal wear and tear excepted. Lessee shall be responsible for all repairs required, excepting the roof, exterior walls, and structural foundations.

As you can probably see already, there are many potential problems with this clause. You may have a hard time getting a landlord to change some of these requirements. While it is acceptable for them to ask you to fix any problems you may have caused, such as damage to walls, the idea that you are responsible for heating and cooling systems is a bit troublesome. This could run into very costly repairs. In addition, the lease does not state what responsibility the landlord has to fix such problems. Ask that this section be made much more specific, with phrases such as "normal wear and tear" defined explicitly.

In addition, you might want to double check with your insurance company to be sure that if the roof leaks you would be covered under their policy. If not, will you be covered for any loss under the landlord's policy and what is the system for recourse?

4. Alterations

Lessee shall not, without first obtaining written consent of Lessor, make any additions, alterations, or improvements to the premises.

Again, this is way too vague. What is their definition of an addition or alteration? If you put in slat walls to display your merchandise, is that considered a violation of the contract? Ask for some more specifics here. The inability to add display fixtures could really hinder your business. Do not wait until after you have signed the contract to find out you can't create the store you have envisioned because of a clause in the lease agreement.

5. Ordinances and Statutes

Lessee shall comply with all ordinances, statues and requirements of state, federal and local authorities.

This is pretty much a given and you really have no choice but to do this anyway.

6. Subletting

Lessee shall not assign or sublet any portion of this lease or premises without prior written consent of the Lessor, which shall not be unreasonably withheld. Any such assignment or subletting without consent shall be void and may terminate this lease.

This is pretty straightforward and standard.

7. Utilities

All applications and connections for utility services on the stated premises shall be made in the name of the Lessee only, and Lessee shall be solely liable for utility charges as they become due, including charges for gas, water, sewer, electricity, and telephone.

This, too, is standard. It is your responsibility to cover your utilities with most landlords. There are a few who will cover some costs. It depends on the building and the landlord.

8. Entry and Inspections

Lessee will permit Lessor or agents of Lessor to enter the premises during reasonable times and with notice and will permit the Lessor to post "For Lease" signs within ninety (90) days prior to the expiration of this lease.

This is pretty standard, however, try to get a specific statement about what type of notice, how the Lessee will receive the notice and what constitutes reasonable times (i.e. regular business hours). It is also standard to allow them to place "For Lease" signs sixty days prior to the expiration of the contract. This is not a major point, but you may want to request it, if you feel the signs might hinder your business in any way.

9. Indemnification of Lessor

The Lessor will not be held liable for any damage or injury to Lessee, or any other person, or property occurring on the stated premises. Lessee agrees to not hold Lessor liable for any damages regardless of how they are caused.

This section is troubling. What if the Lessor knows there is a structural fault with the building, does not fix it and you or one of your customers are harmed? Get the landlord to strike this clause or have it changed.

10. Insurance

Lessee shall retain public liability and property damage insurance at the Lessee's own cost.

This is standard, and you will want this anyway. Some contracts may go on further and state the exact types of coverage you will need and/or amounts. Some will require proof of insurance.

11. Destruction of Property

Should the premises be destroyed in part or whole, Lessor shall repair the property within sixty (60) days. Lessee shall be entitled to a deduction in rent during the time the repairs are taking place. If there are repairs which cannot be made within sixty (60) days, this lease may be terminated at the request of either party.

You will want this standard clause, as well. If your space is compromised, you want the landlord to repair the defect as quickly as possible. Otherwise, you could lose business indefinitely. If they are not able to make the repairs in a timely manner, you have the option of terminating the lease and moving your store elsewhere.

12. Nonpayment of Rent

If Lessee defaults on regular payment of rent, or defaults on the other conditions herein, Lessor may give Lessee notice of the default and if the Lessee does not cure the default within thirty (30) days, after receiving written notice of the default, Lessor may terminate this lease.

This is pretty simple. If you do not pay your rent, then the landlord reserves the right to ask you to remove your store from the premises. You may want to try to get sixty days instead of thirty but there is not much wiggle room with this clause.

13. Security Deposit

Lessee shall pay a security deposit upon the signing of this lease to Lessor for the sum of 600 dollars ($600.00). Lessor shall keep the full amount of the security deposit available throughout the term of this lease.

Although a security deposit equaling the first month's rent is pretty standard, I would want to see a bit more detail here about how and under what conditions this money will be returned to the Lessee. This is pretty vague and you may wind up not getting your deposit back. Landlords have been known to make up phony repair or cleaning charges so they can keep your deposit.

14. Attorney's Fees

In the event of a suit being brought for recovery of the premises, or for any sum due under the conditions of this contract, the prevailing party shall be entitled to reimbursement of all costs, including but not limited to attorney's fee.

15. Notices

All notices to either party shall be provided in writing at the address listed on this contract.

Both clauses 14 and 15 are standard.

16. Option to Renew

As long as Lessee is not in default of this lease, Lessee shall have the option of renewing the lease for an additional term of twelve (12) months starting upon the expiration of the term of the original lease. All the terms and conditions herein outlined shall apply during the extension. This option can be implemented by giving written notice to the Lessor at least ninety (90) days prior to the expiration.

I would try for sixty days prior on the notice. You may be looking for another place and not quite sure if you are moving out in three months.

17. Entire Agreement

The preceding makes up the entire agreement between the parties and may only be modified by agreement of both parties in writing.

Signed this ___ day of ________, 20__.

____

Ima Yogurtseller, Lessee

____

Big Commercial Landlord, Lessor

4.2 Store Design

Once you have chosen your space, you will need to decorate the inside and outside. To help you in this task, you may want to start by choosing a "theme" for your store. Once you have decided on a theme, you can choose your store layout, logo, background music, lighting, and even scents that will pull your store and its theme together.

Will your store be contemporary or old-fashioned? Will it be hip and young, relaxing, or upscale? It is important to choose an atmosphere that will draw customers into your store and reflect the type of merchandise you plan to offer.

Ambiance is an especially important selling feature for food service establishments. Customers often patronize food establishments not only for their menu selection but for the setting. Careful selection of fixtures, furnishings, furniture, and other design elements can help you to create the desired ambiance of your ice cream shop.

4.2.1 Outside the Store

Remember the external appearance of your store is the first impression potential customers have of your business. It should be neat but eye-catching.

Does it need a fresh coat of paint? If the landlord is responsible for outside paint but does not seem in a hurry to finish the project, offer to paint it yourself for a discount on your rent that month. Let's say the paint costs you $30, and it takes you two hours to paint. You figure your time is worth $20 an hour. You would ask the landlord to grant you a seventy dollar credit on that month's rent (arrange this before you paint). Many landlords will work with you on this because it saves them money and the aggravation of hiring an outside contractor. Your bonus is a fresh coat of paint to hang your new, bright sign upon.

Signage

After your choice of name and location, your choice of signage is probably the most important aspect of creating interest in your location. You will want an eye-catching sign that customers can see from the street. A good sign can actually entice customers into your store. Your signage could mean the difference between bringing foot traffic right to your store or people walking right on by.

Signs are available in a variety of materials and styles. Electric signs offer many advantages, notably that they are bright, colorful, and attractive, and the lighting makes them—and your shop—readily visible. Many municipalities regulate electric signs, so check with your local building department to find out if there are any zoning restrictions and what permits are needed.

The most common electric signs are illuminated signs and neon signs. Illuminated signs are lit from behind by fluorescent lamps or tubes. They generally show the store's name and may include a logo or decorative elements. They are generally posted above a store's door or under the roof line. A professional electric sign builder can custom design and install an illuminated sign. Neon signs are lit glass tubes that can be custom made to show the name of your store, your store's logo, or a picture. Standard neon business signs are also available for words such as Open and Ice Cream.

Another type of electric sign is an LED sign. These come in a variety of sizes, from small indoor displays that sit in the window to large, free-standing signs that can be seen from a distance. Both can display static or changing text, such as to advertise a sale or promotion. Other types of signs include window etchings or paintings, banners, plaques, carved wooden signs, and metal letters.

Your signs should reflect your style. To create more effective and professional-looking signs you might decide to have a sign custom made by a local sign shop in order to create a decorative sign in line with your shop's theme. For example, if you are opening a nostalgic ice cream parlor, you could hang a vintage-looking sign. If you are opening a highly contemporary shop aimed at the 20-35 age group, you might want a funky graphical sign. Make sure your sign can be seen it from a distance and that it clearly shows what your shop is selling.

Logo

With some of today's inexpensive graphics software, it is possible to create your own simple logo and use it on your sign and other business materials. People will come to associate your store with that logo.

There are companies, such as **MyLogo.com** or **LogoYes.com**, that you can pay to create a logo for you. MyLogo.com will create a custom designed logo for you for about $100 for a basic package. With LogoYes.com, you design your own logo using their online template that uses standard clip art. They charge about $50 for a logo design or $100 for a logo with 100 business cards.

You could also purchase software that lets you design your logo on your own. There are a number of different programs like Logo Design Studio (**www.summitsoftcorp.com/products/Logo-Design-Studio**), for example, which sell for less than $50. If you decide you want to design your own logo with this type of software, be sure they offer a demo version that you can try out first, so that you know it meets your needs. Most local print shops also offer design services, since they already have the software for it. Keep in mind that, if you have already chosen a theme, your sign and logo can be a good place to tie into that theme again.

Lettering and Fonts

Make sure the letters on your sign are large enough that customers will be able to spot the words from a distance. If your sign will be more than 400 feet from the street front, then you will want to use seven- to ten-inch high letters. If you are located inside a mall, where you will not need to be visible from a street, then you may be able to use lettering between three and a half to seven inches.

Watch the fonts you use for your sign. A fancy script may look nice, but customers might have a difficult time reading the letters. Use both upper and lowercase letters for some variety and to make the sign easier to read. The colors of the sign should contrast with one another — dark and light colors work best (black and white, yellow and navy blue, white and royal blue).

You might find hiring an expert for this particular job worthwhile even though it will cost you a little extra money. Most small towns have stores that create signs for local businesses. Be sure that you get several quotes for your project, as prices can vary widely. Also, do not rule out buying the sign used. You may be able to locate a simple sign without a store name at a store that is going out of business

Be sure to check with your landlord or city zoning board to find out about any ordinances on signs. Some cities have very specific guidelines about height, placement, and other requirements, particularly if you're in a heritage area where local history is used as a tourism draw. It's better to check with your municipality before investing a lot of money in a sign you can't use. Many municipalities also require a sign permit. Check with your city or town's building department to find out whether a permit is needed.

Also, most malls have specific requirements for store signs, such as requiring a minimum/maximum letter height, lighted signs, etc. If your location comes with a place to install a sign, you will probably be able to order an appropriate sign with the help of the mall's management. Professional sign companies offer design and manufacturing — check in your local Yellow Pages under the "Signs — Commercial" category. Another option is to order a sign online. Here are a few companies that specialize in signs for businesses:

- *Sandblasted Signs*
  www.sandblastedsigns.com

- *Spring Valley Signs*
  www.springvalleysigns.com

- *American Sign Carver*
  www.signcarving.com

- *Custom Hand-Carved Signs by Sally Claus Focht*
  www.customhandcarvedsigns.com

- *Lincoln Signs*
  www.lincolnsign.com

4.2.2 Inside the Store

Interior design is really one of the most enjoyable parts of opening your own store. There is nothing like planning and preparing for your store, and then suddenly seeing it ready, in all its glory, just waiting for the first customer to step through the door. Planning your space helps you create an environment that customers will love and enjoy being in.

Creating a space that customers love will encourage them to buy — and to return again. Your layout will depend upon a variety of factors, such as the space available, the shape of that space and the amount of items you have available.

To design the interior space of your store, imagine your store full of customers. What are their needs? What are their expectations? What sort of design elements will help your customers move through your door, enjoy the process of shopping in your store, and have a positive experience purchasing what they want? How can you set up a functional store interior that will help them get what they want and leave, happily anticipating their next return trip?

Service Counter Area

Customers tend to head to the service counter when they enter an ice cream shop. Keep that space open and allow ample room for crowds. Setting the service counter far back from the front entrance allows room for customers to wait in line. Think about the possible layouts and how you want the traffic to flow through the store. Be sure to leave plenty of room around the cash register in case you have several customers in the store at once. Customers also like to view the food selections, so make the area in front of the service counter wide enough so they can browse behind customers who are being waited on. If you offer ice cream products in a display case, set it near but off to the side of the service counter. That way you can keep your eyes on it and offer assistance if needed.

Make your service counter appealing and functional. The employee side of the service counter should provide ample room for employees to move and prepare products. Plan for extra space so there is room for additional employees during busy periods. Determine what equipment and supplies are needed and design the layout to facilitate food preparation. Include room for storage of extra supplies and products. Include a display case of your ice creams and toppings for customer view, but be sure to separate it from the customers with a clear partition or food shield.

If you plan to have seating, set it far enough away from the service counter and line area so that it does not obstruct customers waiting to be served. Setting tables close to the window allows customers to have a view as they eat and helps to attract passersby to your store as they view customers enjoying your products.

Cash Register Area

Make your cash desk appealing and functional. Your cash register should be in a spot where you can greet customers as they come into the store, while allowing you to keep an eye on the rest of the store. Do not overcrowd the checkout area. Keep in mind your customers may have their arms loaded with items and will want a place to set them down. You should have a worktop that allows enough room for placing purchases and also some napkins and plastic utensils.

Walls

Your walls can be used to create an ambiance, or carry out your theme, and as a marketing tool. If your shop is an old-fashioned ice cream parlor, you can display nostalgic photos and memorabilia. If your shop offers homemade organic ice cream, you may want to hang a photo of a dairy cow being milked along with posters about the health advantages of organic ice cream and the ice cream supplier.

Your walls can also be used to promote your own products. Artful photos and posters showing your menu items is often the best in-store promotion possible. Customers appreciate having a visual image of menu items, which can speed time needed to make a selection and order once at the service counter. Such pictures can also entice customers to select specific items. For example, a customer may plan to order a single scoop of ice cream and decide on a hot fudge sundae after seeing a picture of rivulets of hot fudge cascading over two scoops of ice cream and topped by delectable looking swirls of whipped cream and sprinkles of nuts.

Other possibilities for using wall space include creating a photo board of customers eating your ice cream selection and a bulletin board posted with community announcements and store promotions.

Store Layout

As you will see from the sample store layout, it is important that the traffic in your store be able to flow from point A to point B. You can print or photocopy the samples below to create a mock-up of your own retail space to help you with designing a layout that works well for your store.

Your entry should be open and inviting. The service area should be readily visible, and it should be clear to customers where to order or line up. If products are sold in a display case or freezer, it should be clear where such items are located.

If there is a crowd, is there room for them to pass one another? What about wheelchairs or other special needs? The layout of your store can affect how long a customer stays and how many items they purchase. Have you ever been in an ice cream shop where a large, noisy crowd is jammed inside with hordes of people waiting outside? Depending on your level of patience and desire for ice cream, you either stayed or left. Do not let your store become so crowded that it turns customers away or creates a bad impression.

Sample Store Layout

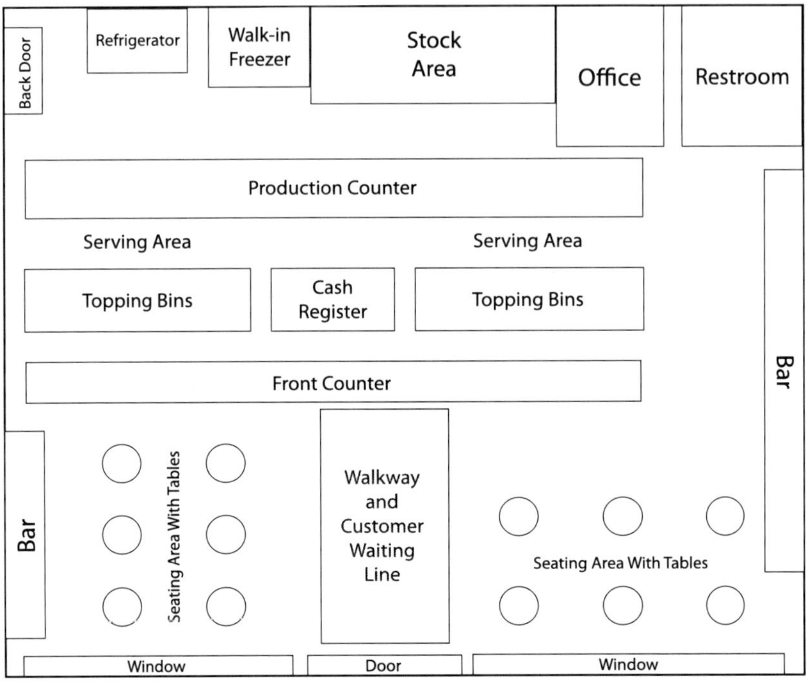

Keep aisles clear and easy to move through. Be sure there is ample space in the seating area for customers to sit comfortably and without feeling cramped or interfering with customers in line. Provide seating areas for individuals, such as a bar or long table, as well as groups. If possible, set a few tables apart from the busiest part of the store's activity for customers with wheelchairs or those desiring a quieter environment.

If space is limited, you may want to ask customers with baby strollers to leave them outside. Post a sign and make a space available in front of the store's windows where patrons can keep an eye on them.

Another consideration is all the point-of-sale and other equipment and retail supplies you will need at your cash desk. Make sure there is space behind your counter for credit card processing machines, your computer, bags, and other sales aids. Your cash desk will likely need to have shelving and drawers built into it for storage of supplies.

TIP: Be sure to display notices of any special events or sales. You can also put out any promotional materials for customers to take and share with others. Magnetized business cards are a good investment and remind customers of your store each time they go to their refrigerator.

Indoor Lighting

Harsh fluorescent lighting may sound like something you would worry over in an office building, but it can change the look of items you are trying to sell, too. It can make items looks washed out or a different or unappealing color.

Certain types of lighting can also disturb customers and cause them to leave the store sooner than you would like. If you have ever walked into a bookstore with flickering fluorescent lights and tried to read the back cover of a book, you know how irritating this can be. You don't want your customers walking out on you because you chose the wrong lighting.

Lighting in an ice cream shop is especially important because poor lighting can make a place seem dirty or dingy. Use bright light to illuminate the inside of your shop and convey a clean, fresh, airy message.

Be aware of small things like this. You can become so used to them that you are not even aware of the problem. Watch your customers. Be aware of their reactions and ask questions if they seem irritated.

4.2.3 Store Security and Loss Prevention

One of the facts of life in retail is that you can become the target of shoplifters. How you lay out your store is an important component of deterring shoplifting. You need to deter burglars as well and your business insurance policy might require you to install an alarm system. A good alarm system can pay for itself in reduced rates and thwarting would-be thieves.

Security Systems

There are many security companies who can provide you with the equipment and support you'll need to keep your store secure. Check out your local Yellow Pages to find security companies in your area. To learn more about security for your store you can check out ADT Security Systems (**www.adt.com/smbiz**) who offer a variety of services for surveillance and alarms systems for small business owners. Broadview Security is another trusted name in security systems. You can find out about the many services they offer for small businesses at **www.broadviewsecurity-business.com**.

> **TIP:** Check with your landlord to see if they will cover the cost of installation if the alarms are not already provided (you can purchase basic alarms at any hardware or department store).

Not only should you consider having a security system installed, but you need to learn and teach any staff you hire about how to be on the lookout for suspicious behavior. Place a security mirror to reflect corners you can't see from your cash desk. A security camera is also a great idea to aid in apprehending anyone you think might be shoplifting.

Preventing Employee Theft

If all of your merchandise is behind the service counter and customers pay for it in advance of receiving it, you will not need to be concerned with shoplifting. All shop owners, with the exception of owners with no employees, do need to be concerned about employee theft. Employee theft in retail stores is high, with statistics showing that the greatest losses are due to employee thefts and not shoplifters and burglars. According to the University of Florida National Retail Security Survey, retailers in the United States lost $40.5 billion to theft in 2007, with almost half of the losses due to employee theft.

Food service establishments are prone to high product loss both intentionally and inadvertently. Intentional losses involve employees who raid the inventory and help themselves to product, who eat items without paying for them, and who give away free items to friends who shop at the store. Inadvertent losses are due to employees who give away more product than they should due to failure to follow portion controls. Both types of losses can make a huge dent in a store's profits and increase food costs.

Ways to minimize intentional theft include keeping inventory locked up and limiting access to inventory, using sign-out sheets for items taken from inventory or food-storage areas, giving employees an allocation of food giveaways, and monitoring storerooms and inventory closely. To minimize accidental loss, stress the importance of portion control and institute procedures to ensure employees are not over-scooping or giving away excess food.

Monitor inventory against food purchases and projections. If you are ordering food more often than expected, it may be that servers are giving too-large portions. Provide retraining and be sure the proper serving ladles and equipment is available.

4.3 Displaying Merchandise

If you are planning on offering self-service items to take home or non-food items in addition to menu items you will need to display it in a display case or on shelves. While there are many different theories on how a store should be merchandised, the most important thing is to arrange your items to give an organized and clean appearance.

> **TIP:** Look in decorating magazines for ideas for displays in your store. Reading books and magazines about interior design will help you create a style for your shop. Additionally, most community colleges offer night classes in decorating that would help you understand the principles needed to create eye-catching and pleasing displays.

4.3.1 Where to Get Display Fixtures

To find display cases and fixtures for displaying the merchandise you are selling, you can check the Yellow Pages or do an online search for retail fixtures.

Here are a few useful sites to get you started:

- *Ice Cream Equipment World*
  www.icecreamequipmentworld.com/index-dippingdisplaymerchandisers.html

- *Display Warehouse*
  www.displaywarehouse.com

- *Franklin Fixtures*
  www.franklinfixtures.com

- *Victory Display Equipment*
  www.victorydisplay.com

- *Eddies*
  www.eddies.com

Be on the lookout for stores going out of business — do not be afraid to approach them and offer to purchase their display fixtures. You might also consider building the fixtures yourself or hiring someone to do so. For used displays, try publications like The Trader (**www.traderonline.com**), and check out the classifieds in your local newspaper. Do not overlook auction sites like eBay for additional opportunities to pick up display racks at a reasonable price. See section 4.5, "Equipment and Supplies," for more information on display cases.

4.3.2 Maximizing Sales

Where to Place Items

Merchandise with the highest margin of profit should be placed at the front of your store. This way the customer passes it twice—once on the way in, and once on the way out. You want these to jump out and grab customers as they walk in the door and as they walk out. Display these goods in special ways so that they attract attention quickly.

Popular items that most people are looking for (whatever the current trend is) should be placed at the back of the store. That way, people will need to walk through almost your entire inventory in order to get to those pieces. This is exactly why milk is always at the back of the supermarket.

Impulse Displays

Think about the check-out area of your favorite big name stores. "Oh, yes," you say as you stand there waiting for the cashier, "I really need batteries, a book light, and some air freshener." This is called impulse displaying and you can do the same thing. In an ice cream shop, think of the ordering area, rather than the checkout area, as the place to add on impulse items. Place optional items, such as specialty cones or bowls that your customers might normally overlook, closer to your service area in order to pique people's interest and trigger an impulse purchase. Try displaying different items week by week to see what sells best.

4.3.3 Creating Window Displays

If you are fortunate to have a great window with a view to a well-traveled sidewalk, be sure to take advantage of it to make your shop irresistible to passing customers. Traditional window displays of merchandise aren't feasible as ice cream is perishable, but you can create a window display that makes your store seem interesting and inviting.

If your shop is an old-fashioned ice cream parlor, you can add curtains or drapes to create a homey feel. Adding touches like antique ice cream parlor chairs and equipment can re-create the look of a historic ice cream parlor. If your shop makes any products on site, such as Belgian waffle cones, consider moving the equipment to the front of the store. Watching a waffle maker display his craft can be entertaining and attract a crowd and potential customers.

For many shops, the best window display will be a large window that reveals the shop and customers enjoying its wares. If the only merchandise you offer is food products that will be consumed right away, this may be your only option. But be sure that what customers see is inviting. Be aware that you and your shop are on display at all times and keep the store clean, orderly, and ready for business at all times. Potential customers who see store employees lounging around during slow periods, dirty tables, or furniture in disarray may be turned off and go elsewhere. Exciting window displays will encourage customers to come in and browse. Some things to remember:

- Make sure the glass is clean with no streaks. You may have to clean the windows often, particularly if your clientele includes children, but it will be worth the effort.

- Even when you aren't open, you may want to light the window displays to attract new customers who will see the items and come back during regular business hours.

- A few props can go a long way. Think thematically, and try to incorporate things like holidays, special local events or the passing seasons into your displays.

Here's a list of basic ideas to tie in the season with merchandise in your window display (let loose your creativity and imagination from there):

- *Autumn:* Brightly colored leaves and a few large branches with a couple of large pumpkins in the center.
- *Spring:* Flowers and greenery suggest spring. A strategically placed fan can create the impression of a breeze.
- *Summer:* A beach theme is easy with some inexpensive sand, sea shells, and beach balls. (The sand cleans up easily with a shop vacuum.)
- *Winter:* Christmas trees and lights create an eye-catching display. Create a snowy scene using cotton batting or even a white sheet.

Sample Window Display

Let's develop the Belgian waffle maker theme as a window display a little further. You can set up the window display by building a small elevated platform to bring the equipment, supplies, and waffle maker to eye level of passersby. Include a stand for the food preparation materials and another for the cooked cones.

Arrange the cooked cones and cooking supplies in an artful way to attract attention.

You would set the waffle making machine and stand up first. These items should be placed to the left or right of the center of the display window. This will not cause the display to look unbalanced, but will be pleasing to the eye.

Next, you want your focal point to look as nice as possible. Arrange the cooked cones in an artful way and add colorful accessories, such as mixing bowls, measuring cups, and cloths, to make your display more interesting.

The centerpiece of your display will be the waffle maker. Have the person making the waffles wear a colorful costume, such as a chef's jacket and hat, or ethnic clothing if appropriate to your shop's or town's heritage. Instruct your waffle maker to entertain the crowd with dramatic gestures, motions, and flourishes as he or she mixes the batter, ladles it onto the waffle grills, removes the cooked cone and rolls it up.

Finally, keep your waffle-making operations functional. Restock the serving area with cooked cones as needed.

You can also tie in promotional activities with entertainment-style window displays. Crowds may gather to watch your window display but fail to come in the store. Store employees—or even the waffle maker—can go outside to greet people and pass out coupons or other incentives that will help to bring customers into the store.

Entertainment-style window displays work best in tourist areas that have heavy foot traffic and large number of new visitors to an area.

4.4 Obtaining Your Inventory

Your inventory consists of the ice cream and other frozen desserts that you will sell to customers. Ice cream shop owners either purchase their inventory of frozen desserts already made, or make the ice cream or other products themselves.

4.4.1 Buying Ice Cream and Frozen Desserts

Most of the national brands of ice cream and frozen desserts offer wholesale purchasing opportunities. You can find major ice cream suppliers in MacRae's Blue Book, a national directory of wholesalers which is available free of charge online at **www.macraesbluebook.com**.

If you do a search for ice cream at MacRae's Blue Book, you will find suppliers in several categories. While you can look through the almost 900 companies listed under "Ice Cream," you will likely find suitable suppliers of frozen desserts for your shop more quickly by reviewing the much smaller list of suppliers of "Dairy Products: Ice Cream, Bulk."

Many makers of ice cream and frozen desserts will simply sell their products to you at wholesale prices (see box below). However, a few ice cream makers offer arrangements which they may refer to as licensing, partnership, or business opportunities. Such arrangements may be similar to franchising in a number of ways, such as requiring a signed agreement with the company that may restrict your ability to sell other products.

> **TIP:** If you are considering a licensing or partnership arrangement for obtaining your inventory, make sure you investigate thoroughly and review the information in this guide about franchising for advice on what to watch for.

Wholesale Prices and Terms

Wholesalers typically offer discounts based on quantities purchased. Here are some questions to consider when considering their prices and terms:

- Are the prices and terms the company is offering acceptable? Ask the vendor to tell you all the charges that will be involved with a purchase. In addition to the price of the product, there may be taxes, delivery charges, duties for items coming from another country, rush charges, etc. If you are dealing with a wholesaler, you should ask about "up charges" (a fee on top of the manufacturer's price).

- What discount will you receive off the retail price? Typical discounts when buying wholesale are 20-50% (discounts are usually higher when buying direct from the manufacturer because there's nothing being paid to a wholesaler). You may need a copy of your retail license to get the wholesale rate or to avoid paying sales tax.

- When is payment required? If you do not have a business history, most vendors will want to be paid for items before they ship them. Many times you will not be able to purchase wholesale using your credit card, so you will need to have funds readily available to cover your purchases with a check.

- What about over-runs or under-runs? While manufacturers normally do their best to ensure they deliver exactly what you have ordered, many include in their contract that they can ship 10-15% over or under the amount ordered.

TIP: Make sure you read any sales contracts carefully and have them reviewed by your lawyer to ensure you are protected.

4.4.2 Making Your Own Ice Cream or Frozen Desserts

Your other option for obtaining your inventory is to make it yourself. As mentioned earlier in this guide, many shops in specialty niches such "old-fashioned ice cream parlors" and "ethnic" shops offer for sale unique ice cream products they manufacture themselves.

If you do plan to make your own ice cream, make sure you read chapter 2 of this guide, particularly section 2.1.4 which provides an overview of the process of making ice cream including calculating fat content, quantities to make, and adding flavorings. Other sections in chapter 2 offer advice on resources that will help you learn how to make frozen desserts for your shop.

If you make your own ice cream, you will need commercial ice cream making equipment. Commercial ice cream makers can make anywhere from 3 to 9 quarts an hour for a small machine and up to 30 gallons per hour for the larger, pricier models. A small commercial ice cream maker can make a batch of ice cream in about 20 minutes (1 quart up to 3 quarts). You can find links to suppliers of commercial ice cream makers in section 4.5 of this guide.

In addition to an ice cream maker, you will need to buy ingredients for making ice cream. You can save money on your ingredients by purchasing in bulk from a wholesaler. A wholesaler buys products from the manufacturer, usually in large quantities, and resells them in smaller lots to retailers. As a result, the wholesaler is sometimes referred to as the "middleman" between retailers and manufacturers. You will get the best deal if you can buy directly from the manufacturer. However, some may not be willing to sell to you because of their arrangements with their current wholesalers. In those cases, you will need to go to the wholesaler.

Since your products are perishable, you will need to gauge your pre-production inventory carefully so that you don't waste your perishables and your money. Some items, i.e. dry goods like sugar, can be stored for long periods, while others, such as your dairy supplies, will need to be used up quickly. Obviously you can purchase more of the dry goods and not worry too much about over-purchasing.

For wholesale food supplies such as sugar, milk, eggs, etc., check your Yellow Pages under "Grocers Wholesale" to find suppliers in your area. You'll do best to develop a long-term relationship with a nearby supplier you trust. A local supplier will be there to answer your questions and to meet any special needs you might have. National wholesale chains such as Costco are also an option for most of these types of supplies. To find suppliers of specialty ingredients needed to make ice cream and other frozen desserts, see the information about suppliers in section 4.5.2.

4.5 Equipment and Supplies

There are a variety of items you will need to have in your store before you open for business. This section contains a list of suggested equipment for stocking frozen desserts, foodservice items, and other supplies you will need for your business. The list is followed by information about suppliers (companies that can provide the supplies and equipment you will need).

4.5.1 What You'll Need

Following are some of the most common equipment and supplies for ice cream shops. Use this list as a starting point for determining your own needs. Check what your store already has, or what your landlord provides, and make your shopping list based on what type of shop you plan to open.

Your menu items will drive your equipment needs. For example, scoop shops will need equipment for storing and scooping ice cream as well as topping dispensers, cone makers and holders, and whip cream dispensers. Soft serve shops will need soft serve machines; gelaterias will need a gelato/batch ice cream freezer and display case. If you decide to make your own ice cream, you will need a commercial ice cream maker.

Likewise, your shop set-up will determine what type of furniture and foodservice supplies you need. Shops serving sit-down customers, such as in a restaurant or ice cream parlor, will need glass or plastic fountainware and silverware; other shops will need disposable bowls, cups, and silverware.

Equipment and Supplies Checklist

Food Preparation

- ❑ Cone making machine
- ❑ Ice cream blender
- ❑ Ice cream maker
- ❑ Push cart
- ❑ Scales
- ❑ Stainless pans
- ❑ Stainless steel prep tables
- ❑ Waffle maker

Food Service

- ❑ Cold topping bins/bar
- ❑ Cone dispenser
- ❑ Cone holder
- ❑ Dipping well
- ❑ Disposable serving cups and bowls
- ❑ Disposable flatware
- ❑ Flurry blizzard machine
- ❑ Food shields
- ❑ Fountainware (glass or plastic)
- ❑ Gelato display and dipping cases
- ❑ Hot fudge warmer
- ❑ Ice cream scoopers, spades, ice scrapers, and spatulas
- ❑ Ladles and measuring scoops

- ❑ Milkshake machine
- ❑ Napkins
- ❑ Napkin holders
- ❑ Soft serve machine
- ❑ Straws
- ❑ Sundae toppings dispensers
- ❑ Whipped topping dispenser

Storage

- ❑ Cake display freezer
- ❑ Combination Freezer: Soft serve and shake
- ❑ Cone cabinet
- ❑ Display dipping cabinet/freezer
- ❑ Frozen custard freezer
- ❑ Gelato/batch ice cream freezer
- ❑ Ice cream chest freezer
- ❑ Reach-in display freezer
- ❑ Reach-in freezer
- ❑ Reach-in refrigerator
- ❑ Storage containers
- ❑ Walk-in cooler
- ❑ Walk-in freezer
- ❑ Yogurt freezer

Selling Supplies

- ❑ Bags

- ❑ Blank gift certificates
- ❑ Boxes
- ❑ Cash register/POS system
- ❑ Credit card machines
- ❑ Display or menu board
- ❑ Signs ("Sale", "Open/Closed", "Store Hours", etc.)

Office or Employees Only Area

- ❑ Break Room
- ❑ Bulletin board for employee laws and other postings
- ❑ Chairs
- ❑ Coffee maker and coffee supplies
- ❑ Computer
- ❑ Desks
- ❑ FAX machine (optional)
- ❑ Filing cabinets
- ❑ Internet connection
- ❑ Office supplies (pens, paper, stapler, scissors, tape, markers, clips, etc.)
- ❑ Phones with voice mail
- ❑ Printer (consider a combination fax/printer/copier/scanner)
- ❑ Microwave
- ❑ Software
- ❑ Stationery (see section 6.1.3 for more on stationery)
- ❑ Tables

- ❑ Time clock
- ❑ Trash cans

Overall Store

- ❑ Air filters
- ❑ Broom and dust pan
- ❑ Burglar alarm
- ❑ Carpeting or area rugs
- ❑ Chairs
- ❑ Cleaning supplies
- ❑ Commercial dishwasher
- ❑ Fire alarm
- ❑ Fire extinguishers
- ❑ Hand sinks
- ❑ Light bulbs
- ❑ Line stands
- ❑ Mop
- ❑ Paint
- ❑ Tables
- ❑ Trash cans and trash bags
- ❑ Vacuum cleaner
- ❑ Wall decorations
- ❑ Wallpaper
- ❑ Wastebaskets
- ❑ Window treatments (e.g. blinds)

4.5.2 Where to Get Equipment and Supplies

There are numerous suppliers of new and used equipment and furniture for ice cream shops. Many suppliers can be found simply by checking your local Yellow Pages. However, we have included a number of links in this guide to help you with your search for suppliers.

You can find suppliers in the food industry's comprehensive reference directory Food and Beverage Market Place, which is available at many public libraries with Business Reference collections. It also is available online for a subscription fee at **www.foodmp.com/index.php?p=1**. You can also find a number of suppliers listed in MacRae's Blue Book which is available free online at **www.macraesbluebook.com**. A search for ice cream will bring up a variety of manufacturers of freezers, ice cream makers, and other equipment and supplies.

In addition, many trade associations and industry publications publish Buyers Guides and Source Books, both online and in print copies. These directories often include member companies rather than a full list of suppliers. See trade publications, section 2.6.1, for more information. Following are a few specific resources to locate suppliers.

> **TIP:** Be sure that all equipment you purchase is approved by the National Sanitation Foundation (NSF) or Underwriters Laboratories (UL). Both are recommended seals of approval and are also requirements of many local health departments.

Food Service Equipment and Supplies

- *Restaurant Association Buyer's Guide*
  (To access the guide for your state, click on your state on the map, then buyer's guide link.)
  www.restaurant.org/business/buyersguide/index.cfm

- *Foodservice Equipment & Supplies*
  www.restaurant.org/states/index.cfm

- *Food Processing*
  www.foodprocessing.com/articles/2009/equipmentsuppliers.html

- *Food Equipment Association*
  (Click on "Directories & Links" in the "Quick Resources" section)
  www.nafem.org

- *Canadian Restaurant and Foodservices Association Buyers Guide*
  The Buyers Guide offers eight search categories including: Equipment, Furnishings and Supplies; Food & Beverage; Consultants and Services.
  http://buyersguide.crfa.ca/Categories.aspx

- *Hotel & Restaurant Suppliers Association*
  This association offers a search box to locate suppliers in Canada.
  www.afhr.com/en/index.asp

Commercial Ice Cream Making Equipment

- *Ice Cream Professional*
  www.icecreamprofessional.com/comm-ice-cream.php

- *Vieco's Kitchen*
  www.viecokitchen.com/ice.htm

- *PacoJet*
  www.pacojet.com/html/en/pacojet.htm

- *Ice Cream Equipment World*
  www.icecreamequipmentworld.com

Furniture

In addition to the resources below, you can find others by doing an online search for ice cream shop furniture or restaurant furniture.

- *Business.com: Restaurant Furniture*
  www.business.com/directory/food_and_beverage/restaurants_and_foodservice/furnishings/furniture/

- *Foodservice Direct: Restaurant Furniture*
  www.foodservicedirect.com/index.cfm/Restaurant_Furniture.htm

- *Seating Expert*
  www.seatingexpert.com

Cash Registers

You can purchase cash registers that are POS systems, that can be programmed to work with your computer (see section 5.1.4), or you can purchase freestanding systems. You may want to start simple and then upgrade to a deluxe model as your business grows. As with other types of equipment, there are a number of places that you can find used cash registers. You may find new ones at your local office supply store or online through a supplier such as the following:

- *Cash Register Store*
  http://cashregisterstore.com

- *Cash Register Sales, Service and Supply, Inc.*
  www.cashregisterman.com

Retail Supplies

To find supplies used specifically for retail (such as bags, gift certificates, etc.) you can do an online search for retail supplies. Here are a few suppliers to get you started.

- *NEBS*
  www.nebs.com

- *Paper Mart*
  www.papermart.com

- *Bags and Bows*
  www.bagsandbowsonline.com

- *Shopping Bags Direct*
  www.shoppingbagsdirect.com

- *Store Supply Warehouse*
  www.storesupply.com

General Business Supplies

You can find many of the supplies above, as well as office supplies and other business supplies at office supply stores. Office supply chain stores are competitively priced, and may deliver if you buy in quantity.

- *Office Depot*
  www.officedepot.com
- *OfficeMax*
  www.officemax.com
- *Staples*
  www.staples.com

Tips to Save Money

Before you purchase any equipment, carefully consider your requirements. List every product that you plan to sell and identify the equipment for each item. Then, map out where you plan to place each piece of equipment. Many equipment manufacturers will work with you to determine equipment needs and space allocation. For example, you may be able to buy one machine that has dual purposes rather than two machines.

You may also wish to consider leasing equipment. Advantages to leasing include that you put out less money for expensive equipment up front. In the long run, though, leasing can end up costing you more than purchasing the equipment outright.

You also can purchase used equipment. Purchasing used equipment can save you up to 60% of the cost of some items. Be sure to check used equipment out thoroughly and find out when it was originally purchased, how it has been maintained, and any warranties or guarantees offered.

For store fixtures and displays, you might consider building them yourself or hiring someone to do so. For used displays, try publications like The Trader (**www.traderonline.com**), and check out the classifieds in your local newspaper.

Do not overlook auction sites like eBay for additional opportunities to pick up items at a reasonable price. Also be on the lookout for stores going out of business. You can approach them and offer to purchase their display fixtures.

5. Running Your Business

5.1 Store Operations

As you move through the process of opening your store, you will begin to notice that you are starting to develop routines around how you do various things. These routines will fall eventually under the more official business term — operations. One of the great things about owning your own store is that you are in charge of deciding the routines of your operations, and you can plan how things run in your store to satisfy your needs and desires.

Every time you do something new, keep a record of how you did it. As you go along, take accurate notes about what works, what doesn't work, and what will need to be done a different way. Over time you will begin to see an organized system emerge — this is the beginning of the development of your operational procedures.

5.1.1 Developing a Procedures Manual

Having written records and instructions of important store procedures and tasks makes it possible for your employees to complete tasks more efficiently by themselves. Also, store procedures aren't necessarily things that you can (or even want to) store in your head. It is hard to remember all the passwords and codes for things, the procedures for opening and closing the store, or the steps in receiving merchandise. The best thing to do is to make a guide for employees (and for you) to keep this information organized and accessible.

Putting together an operations manual for your store will help you get all of your procedures and instructions for every little task organized and in one spot for you and your employees to refer to. Follow the simple directions below to make your own Store Operations Manual.

What You Need

Here are the things you'll need to create your manual:

- Checklists for each area of the store (see below for some sample checklists)
- Three-ring binder or folder with clear plastic insert space on cover and spine
- Three-hole punch
- Binder dividers with section labels
- Checklist forms
- Task forms
- Special reminder forms
- Emergency forms

What to Do

Once you have gathered your materials, follow these steps:

- Carefully consider each area of your operations. Make divider tags for the binder with the following labels: Opening Tasks, Closing Tasks, Daily Tasks, Weekly Tasks, Monthly Tasks, Quarterly Tasks, Annual Tasks. Place these labeled dividers in the binder.
- Make a checklist for each area. Use the checklist examples on the following pages to get started. List the tasks that you can think of for each area. Remember to write down important reminder information like where things are located, which lights to turn on, etc. Think about how you would instruct someone unfamiliar with the task to do it. Sequentially ordered steps work the best.
- Fill out a separate sequential form or reminder sheet for each specific area of operations in your store.
- Make a list of emergency number and other emergency information for the first page of the binder. You might want to place a copy of every employee's emergency information card inside the binder directly behind the emergency number and procedure page.
- Label the binder clearly and make a copy of all the contents to store in a safe place away from your store.

TIP: Remember that this operations manual will be fluid and will change over time. As you change your procedures, remember to change the corresponding task page.

5.1.2 Areas of Operations Checklists

Here are some examples of various areas of the store and some things in each area that you might want to include in your operations manual:

Opening/Closing

- ❑ Door locks
- ❑ Lights — both indoor and outdoor
- ❑ Security systems and codes
- ❑ What to do if the alarm goes off accidentally

- ❑ Turning on/off the air-conditioning and heating units
- ❑ Turning on/off computers/fax/postal machine/copier
- ❑ Mail sorting and opening
- ❑ Brewing coffee
- ❑ Email
- ❑ Answering machine
- ❑ Clean tables, chairs, and floor.
- ❑ Clean customer restroom.
- ❑ Cleaning break room and staff kitchen area

Cash

- ❑ Operating the cash register
- ❑ Preparing money drawer for opening
- ❑ Processing credit and debit cards
- ❑ Processing checks
- ❑ Accepting and selling gift certificates
- ❑ Completing a transaction
- ❑ Keeping track of what is sold/inventory
- ❑ Phone procedures
- ❑ Directions to store
- ❑ Using computers/fax/postal machine/copier
- ❑ Mailing list
- ❑ Promotions and sales

- ❑ Cash deposits and bank deposits
- ❑ Wrapping gifts

Production Area – Opening Duties

- ❑ Turn on lights
- ❑ Turn on equipment
- ❑ Check freezers and refrigerators are working properly
- ❑ Check ice cream containers and restock
- ❑ Bring out mixes; fill machines
- ❑ Restock ice cream cones
- ❑ Uncover toppings and refill
- ❑ Fill sundae topping dispensers
- ❑ Turn on hot fudge topping dispenser
- ❑ Check display case and restock
- ❑ Check refrigerator items (e.g., whipping cream, cherries) and restock
- ❑ Turn on waffle maker
- ❑ Check stock of paper and plastic supplies
- ❑ Set ladles in topping bins
- ❑ Turn on water for dipping well
- ❑ Set out ice cream scoopers
- ❑ Check shop—including restroom—cleaned thoroughly. Clean any dirty areas.

Production Area – Closing Duties

- ❑ Turn off equipment
- ❑ Clean out milkshake and other machines
- ❑ Check temperature of freezer/display cases
- ❑ Scrape down ice cream containers
- ❑ Turn off water in dipper well and clean
- ❑ Turn off hot fudge dispenser
- ❑ Cover all toppings
- ❑ Refill sundae topping dispensers as needed
- ❑ Clean sundae toppings dispenser
- ❑ Restock paper and plastic supplies
- ❑ Clean inside of ice chest
- ❑ Clean toppings bin
- ❑ Wash all scoopers, spades, and other utensils
- ❑ Wash and sanitize all surface areas: countertops, display panels, cabinets, etc.
- ❑ Hose down floor in service area
- ❑ Wash store floor
- ❑ Empty trash
- ❑ Clean customer restroom

Safety/Health/Emergency Procedures

- ❑ Emergency contact numbers—fire, police, hospitals, etc
- ❑ Staff and owner emergency contact numbers

- ❑ Procedures for emergency in-store illness—for both staff members and customers
- ❑ Evacuation procedures
- ❑ Emergency or natural disaster plan
- ❑ What to do in case of shoplifting
- ❑ What to do in case of robbery

5.1.3 Developing a Product Manual

Putting together a product manual for your store will help you to identify production and quantity standards for each menu item. It also provides a valuable tool for employees to see what a product should look like and portion sizes. Follow the simple directions below to make your own Product Manual.

What You Need

Here are the things you'll need to create your manual:

- Three-ring binder or folder with clear plastic insert space on cover and spine
- Three-hole punch
- Binder dividers with section labels
- Plastic sheet protector
- Digital camera
- Pictures of each product

These can be images taken with a digital camera and printed out on your computer or by a photo developer.

What to Do

Once you have gathered your materials, follow these steps:

- Create a product sheet for each menu item. If an item has more than one size, show both sizes on the same product sheet.
- Include the product's name (e.g., ice cream sundae), a photo of it, and a written description detailing the ingredients, preparation, and serving instructions. For example, a product sheet for an ice cream sundae would show two pictures: a small ice cream sundae and a medium ice cream sundae.

  The following description would appear under the photo of the small sundae:

  > "One four-ounce scoop of ice cream in a small bowl with two squirts of sundae topping (hot fudge, chocolate, strawberry, or caramel), topped by four full whirls of whipped cream, half a teaspoon of peanuts, and one cherry."

  The following description would appear under the photo of the medium sundae:

  > "Two four-ounce scoops of ice cream in a medium bowl with four squirts of sundae topping (hot fudge, chocolate, strawberry, or caramel), topped by four full whirls of whipped cream, half a teaspoon of peanuts, and one cherry."

- Label the dividers with product categories (e.g., sundaes, shakes, blizzards, ice cream cones and bowls). Place these labeled dividers in the binder.
- Place each product sheet in a plastic sheet protector.
- Organize all of the photos by product type and place in the binder.

5.1.4 Inventory Software and POS Systems

Ask ten different ice cream shop owners what inventory system they use to track sales and you will likely get ten different answers. There are a few owners still keeping track of items by hand; however, eventually most retail stores have to use some sort of software as sales volumes increase.

There are a wide variety of options available to store owners. Which software works best is often a personal choice and depends on the type of store, the size of store, and how many customers you have.

Price Labels

Most ice cream shops selling merchandise such as frozen novelties, packaged ice cream, or ice cream cakes usually post the prices on the display case rather than adhering a price label to each item. If you choose to label each item, you can use either simple labels with neat, handwritten prices or printed price stickers from a pricing gun or computer printer.

Some store owners use bar code tags that work with whatever type of software and scanner they are using. It sounds expensive, and initially it might be, but if you sell high quantities of self-serve items, the time you save keeping track of your inventory might pay for it.

Many food service outlets now use POS (point of sales or point of service) systems, which are electronic cash registers that can be used for ordering, recording sales, and tracking inventory. POS systems are custom-designed to match a restaurant's menu items and needs, and range from simple systems with a few functions to complex ones that integrate multiple functions, such as accounting, forecasting, purchasing, and employee scheduling.

This is a big investment, so take your time. Fortunately, many of these POS systems and software programs offer a free demo trial period, so you can try out several different versions before deciding which one you would like to purchase. Try the various demos. Find out which program works best for you before using up valuable hours punching in information on products, only to realize the software you purchased is not working to meet your needs.

> *"When looking for software, try before you buy! Take advantage of the various free demos and talk to the people supporting it. The typical user wants, and needs, the availability of program updates and ongoing assistance when needed."*
>
> — Bill Hawkins, Computer Consultants Exchange

There are several POS systems that stand out as easy to use and filled with great features. Here are just a few of the choices available to you in a range of prices:

- *Halo Point of Sale Program*
  This company offers restaurants in the United States and Canada secure web-based point-of-sale systems. Its website offers informational articles about POS systems and restaurant tips. It also offers webinars, or online training seminars, and live online communication with a consultation. To learn more about its products and request a free demo go to **www.myhalo.com**.

- *NEC Retail Solutions*
  This company offers simple POS systems for fast food and quick service restaurants. To learn more about POSs and how its systems can help you, go to **www.necpos.com**.

- *Assured Computing Technologies*
  Offers point of sale hardware and software for restaurants. Pricing for custom packages vary and include hardware (computer, cash register replacement, and modem) as well as custom-designed software tailored to your store's products. Packages for quick-service restaurants start around $2899. Request information and a quote at **www.assuredcomptech.com**.

5.2 Pricing Your Products

5.2.1 Guidelines

One main consideration for pricing items is what the local market will bear. If certain items are in high demand then you'll probably be able to charge higher prices for those. This is the "law" of supply and demand and you should pay close attention to any trends you see developing in your customers' buying patterns to take advantage of this.

Here are some basic tips for pricing your items:

- Consider what the market will bear. A store in an upscale area may allow you to price your items a bit higher.

- Consider your competition. Are there any other stores like yours in the area? What are they charging for similar items?

- It is not always best to price items lower than the competition charges. Most people believe you get what you pay for. The key is to price the item fairly but allow yourself a reasonable profit.
- Items in a particular section of the retail industry have a certain perceived value. What are customers willing to pay for the item? What is it worth to them?

Another trick most stores use is to price things just under the dollar mark. For example, instead of putting a price of $5.00 on an item, you would mark it $4.99. Even though there is only a penny's difference between the two prices, customers will perceive one as five dollars and the other as four dollars, resulting in better sales.

5.2.2 Retail Pricing Formulas

> *"When we opened in 2001, I was extremely concerned about Mt. Prospect and the surrounding towns not being willing to purchase a gourmet ice cream at a super-premium cost. We kept the prices lower and took a hit our first year because of those concerns. What I realized is that no matter where you are, if you serve a QUALITY product with exceptional service, people will pay for it. It is when you serve a less superior product and/or less than perfect customer service, the customers will be few and far between."*
>
> — Katie Dolan Dix, owner, Capannari Ice Cream

There are different methods that retailers use to arrive at their prices. One of the most efficient and profitable ways to price is using a retail pricing formula. Generally, there are two concepts retailers should be aware of: percentage margin and price markup. Using these formulas will tell you what your percentage of profit is based on the percentage markup above your wholesale (i.e. purchase) price for that item. If the profit percentage is too low, then you'll want to use a different price markup percentage for that item.

As an example of how pricing affects your business, we'll use the break-even point for a fictional business. You may remember the formula for calculating the break-even point from section 3.4.2 as:

Break-even point =
Total fixed costs ÷ (1 – total variable costs ÷ revenues)

In the example in section 3.4.2, the break-even point for the business was $69,000 in annual revenues. Also, for every dollar of sales, the company had 56 cents in variable expenses. Therefore, to break even, fixed costs can represent no more than 44 cents on every dollar. So if you had an item priced at $1.00, 56% of the selling price would be variable expenses and the rest would be fixed costs, leaving no room for profit. Obviously, nobody wants to run their store like that.

Based on these figures, the store owner might want to increase the profit margin. So for example, instead of selling a product for $1.00 as before, the owner might increase the retail price to $1.25. This would lower the percentage for each of fixed and variable costs as a percentage of revenue, resulting in an increased profit margin.

5.2.3 Profit Margin vs. Percentage Markup

Every retailer needs to understand the difference between profit margin and percentage markup. The profit margin is the amount of your retail price that represents profit for you over and above the cost of the merchandise. In a more sophisticated model, you would also include your total operating expenses as well. You would add in your fixed and variable costs and factor them into your pricing model, along with cost of goods.

The percentage markup is the percentage amount you increased the retail price over your cost for a given item. After you have been in business for a while, you will know what price markup generally works best for you. Pricing by percentage markup is less usual than pricing by profit margin.

Let's look at a specific example. Consider an item with a retail price of $1.00, that the owner paid 40 cents for.

The profit margin formula is:

$$\begin{aligned} \text{Margin} &= (1 - (\text{cost} \div \text{selling})) \times 100 \\ &= (1 - (40 \div 100)) \times 100 \\ &= (1 - .40) \times 100 \\ &= .60 \times 100 \\ &= 60 \end{aligned}$$

So in this example the profit margin is 60%.

If, however, you decided that you would set your prices by marking up everything by 60%, then the percentage markup formula is:

$$\begin{aligned} \text{Price} &= \text{cost} + (\text{cost} \times 60 \div 100) \\ &= 40 + (40 \times 0.60) \\ &= 40 + 24 \\ &= 64 \end{aligned}$$

Using a fixed markup of 60%, the retail price on an item costing $0.40 would be $0.64.

Standard Markups

In general, food costs in the restaurant industry are 20–35 percent of the selling price of an item. For example, a serving of salmon that costs $3.00 would sell for $15.00. This represents a 500 percent markup. Below are the basic rules of thumb for marking up some of the items you may sell in your shop:

- *Ice cream:* Mark up by 100 to 300 percent, depending on the type and market. An ice cream cone that cost $1 would therefore sell for $2 to $4 retail.
- *Frozen yogurt:* Mark up by 300 to 600 percent. A small bowl of frozen yogurt with toppings that cost $0.60 wholesale would sell for $2.40 to $3.60 retail.
- *Shaved ice:* Mark up by 800 percent over wholesale cost. A serving of shaved ice that costs $0.22 wholesale can sell for $2 retail.

Sample Price List

Ice Cream and Frozen Desserts

Item:	Cost:
Frozen yogurt w/topping	$3.95 (small); $4.95 (medium); $5.95 (large)
Ice cream cone or bowl	$2.50 (one scoop); $4 (two scoops)
With waffle cone add:	$1.00
Sundae	$4.25 (one scoop); $5.50 (two scoops)
Milk shake	$3.95 (small); $5.45 (medium); $6.95 (large)
Ice cream soda	$4.50
Blizzard	$5.45 (medium); $6.95 (large)
Smoothie	$3.95 (small); $5.45 (medium); $6.95 (large)
Parfait	$5.95 (medium); $6.95 (large)

Look carefully at these two formulas. Notice that markup pricing and profit margin pricing create two very different selling prices. In the first example, pricing based on a 60% profit margin required a selling price of $1.00. In the second example, using a percentage markup of 60% on cost resulted in a price of only 64 cents, a profit margin of only about 38%.

A quick way to calculate a profit margin price is to divide the cost price by the difference between 100 and the profit margin. For example, if you wanted to have a 5% profit margin you would divide your cost price by (100-5) or 95 percent. So if you paid 40 cents for a product and you wanted a 5% profit margin, to arrive at your selling price you would use the formula: 40/(100-5) = 40/.95 = 42 cents. Here are some additional examples so you can see the trend:

10%:	40 ÷ (100 - 10) = 44 cents
15%:	40 ÷ (100 - 15) = 47 cents
25%:	40 ÷ (100 - 25) = 53 cents
50%:	40 ÷ (100 - 50) = 80 cents

Once you know your cost of doing business, you can easily arrive at a minimum profit percentage margin price that will meet your needs. You'll also be able to look at a MSRP and determine if it meets your profit margin requirements.

Keep some of the other pricing concepts in mind as well. Your market may be able to support a higher profit margin in your pricing. Alternatively, you might be able to split margins by pricing higher ticket, lower volume items at a lower profit percentage, and use a higher profit margin on merchandise that sells for a lower price but at a higher volume. Another way to increase your profit margin is to reduce your variable expenses. If you find that your profit margin is too low, you can reduce costs like labor, store supplies, or even look for lower cost wholesale merchandise.

To read more about retail pricing concepts, try the following online resources:

- *Markup or Margin: Selling and Pricing*
  www.buildingtrade.org.uk/articles/markup_or_margin.html

- *Margin Markup/Profit Percentage Table*
  www.csgnetwork.com/marginmarkuptable.html

- *Pricing Your Products and Services Profitably*
  (Click on "Financial Management Series" and look for #7.)
  www.sba.gov/tools/resourcelibrary/publications/index.html

5.3 Getting Paid

As soon as you establish your business you will need to open a business checking account at a bank, trust company, or credit union. You can shop around to find a financial institution that is supportive of small business, or use the same one that you use for your personal banking.

In addition to your checking account, a financial institution may provide you with a corporate credit card used to make purchases for your business, a line of credit to purchase items for your store, and a merchant credit card account enabling you to accept credit card payments from customers.

You have a variety of options for getting paid by your customers.

5.3.1 Accepting Debit Cards

With a debit purchase, the funds come directly out of the customer's account at the bank and are deposited directly into your business bank account. There is no credit involved for customer or merchant. In order to set up debit payment, you will need to ask your bank for an application and you will need a debit machine. The equipment costs about $200 to $500, but some companies offer leases.

There may be a short delay or small charge to you, initially or ongoing, depending on the bank. And you will have to get the equipment to process the payments and print receipts. (Federal law mandates receipts be provided to customers for debit card purchases.) To find out more about debit card services in the U.S., visit the Electronic Transactions Association directory of member companies at **www.electran.org** (click on "Information Resources" then "Links"), or in Canada, visit the Interac Association at **www.interac.ca**.

5.3.2 Accepting Credit Cards

American Express and Discover cards set up merchant accounts nationally and internationally. MasterCard and Visa are local. To become a merchant accepting MasterCard and Visa, you will have to get accepted by a local acquirer (a financial institution like a bank licensed by the credit card company). Because yours is a new business, you may have to shop around to find one that gives you good rates (you may be charged between 1.5 and 3 percent per transaction for the service, and often an initial setup fee and perhaps ongoing fees for phone calls, postage, statements, and so on).

You might also have to provide evidence of a good personal financial record to set up an advantageous rate, at least until you've become established in your business and have a good track record for them to look at. Remember, the bank is granting you credit in this instance, "banking" on the fact that your customers will not want refunds or that you won't try to keep the money if they do.

These days, although the acquiring bank will be a local bank somewhere, it need not be in your hometown. Numerous services are available online to help you set up a merchant account. MasterCard and Visa accounts, as well as American Express and Discover, can all be set up through your local bank or by going to the websites of each of these companies.

- *MasterCard Merchant*
  U.S.: **www.mastercard.com/us/merchant**
  Canada: **www.mastercard.com/ca/merchant/en/index.html**

- *Visa*
  U.S.: **http://usa.visa.com/merchants/merchant_resources/**
  Canada: **www.visa.ca/en/merchant/**

- *American Express*
  U.S.: **https://home.americanexpress.com/homepage/merchant_ne.shtml?**
  Canada: **www10.americanexpress.com/sif/cda/page/0,1641,14821,00.asp**

- *Discover*
  www.discovernetwork.com/discovernetwork/howitworks/howitworks.html

5.3.3 Accepting Checks

Most fast-food and quick-service ice cream shops do not accept checks. If you are opening an ice cream parlor or shop with wait service, you may want to offer customers the option to pay by check. When you accept checks, you may want to have a back-up system for getting paid if the customer has insufficient funds in their checking account. It's important to get a credit card number, driver's license number, and full phone number and address (you might even want to check it online quickly to insure they are legitimate). If you have any doubts as to their honesty, it might be a good idea not to accept the check and let the sale go.

You can accept checks from customers with greater assurance by using a check payment service such as TeleCheck. TeleCheck compares checks you receive with a database of over 51 million bad check records, allowing you to decide whether to accept a check from a particular client. The company also provides electronic payment services, from telephone debit card processing to electronic checks. You can find out more about TeleCheck at **www.telecheck.com**.

5.4 Financial Management

5.4.1 Bookkeeping

We did not speak to a single store owner who enjoyed keeping books, but all of them stressed the importance of doing so. Maintaining accurate, up-to-date records can help you run your business more cost-effectively and efficiently. By keeping track of how much everything costs, you'll quickly know what marketing efforts don't pay off, and what types of pieces are not worth bringing in.

Keeping your books includes tracking two things:

- How much money you have coming in
- How much money you have going out

Bookkeeping Systems

Some people prefer to keep track of everything manually. Many business owners simply buy a few journals, write their accounts across the top and enter each month's expenses by hand. This method works well if you are organized, and love the feel of pen on paper. But if you have employees, several sources of income, and a steady flow of traffic through your store, you'll soon forget a few months, and it will become a monster lying in wait for you in your desk's bottom drawer.

Luckily for small business owners, there are several fairly inexpensive software systems that can easily guide you through the bookkeeping process. Intuit offers different types of financial software for different types of businesses. Intuit's Quickbooks, one of the most popular bookkeeping systems, can run about $800 with point of sale functions, but will quickly pay for itself in the savings of not hiring a full-time bookkeeper. Intuit also offers a basic program, Quicken Home & Business, which is a good option for new businesses and costs about $80.

Many restaurants use software that helps them track their menu items and food costs. Restaurant.com offers a free downloadable set of Microsoft Excel spreadsheets at **www.restaurantowner.com/public/900.cfm**.

Another maker of business management software is Acclivity (formerly MYOB). Their "Premier Accounting" suite allows you to track revenues and expenses, record bank deposits, generate reports, track customers and more. There are several other financial programs, including Accpac and Simply Accounting which you can find at your local office supplies store.

- *Acclivity Premier Accounting*
  www.myob-us.com/premier/

- *Quicken*
  http://quicken.intuit.com

- *Quickbooks*
  http://quickbooks.intuit.com

- *Simply Accounting*
  www.simplyaccounting.com

Even though software can make most of the work easier for you, you might consider taking a beginning accounting or a bookkeeping class at a local community college. Accounting basics are vital information that all store owners need, but sometimes neglect to learn. Even if you hire someone to do your books, you'll need to know the basics so that you can understand what is going on in your accounts.

You might consider hiring a part-time bookkeeper on a contract basis if you find yourself so busy running your store that you don't have time to do your books yourself. Depending on how busy you are, it may take the bookkeeper a few hours per week to get your books up to date and balance them with your bank statements. You can find a bookkeeper through word of mouth or the Yellow Pages.

Even if you plan on having a fulltime bookkeeper or accountant, you should know enough about your store's books to be able to do them yourself if you need to, and certainly to be able to check the accuracy and honesty of those whom you employ. You should know how to:

- Make a daily sales report of how much money you take in every day
- Make accounts payable and accounts receivable reports
- Make and read an income statement (also called a profit and loss statement)
- Make and read a cash flow statement
- Understand a balance sheet

The following sections will help you to understand more about these business basics.

5.4.2 Financial Statements and Reports

"The biggest mistake I see new ice cream shop owners make is not being prepared when they open and cutting corners in service, quality and standards. You want to run your store like any Fortune 500 company. Top quality and attention to detail will set you apart. You need to know your financials three years out and factor in for a disaster or two. So many people do not think past the first year and go off of a wing and a prayer. You need one-year, three-year, and five-year goals in writing and in numbers before you open your doors."

— Katie Dolan Dix, owner, Capannari Ice Cream

The Daily Sales Report

Every day you take in money. You get cash, you take credit cards, and possibly debit cards for payment, and you may even accept checks. A daily sales report logs all of this information. It will also help you ready the monies you take in for your bank deposit. Most accounting software will allow you to enter this information. Some booksellers do this by hand—they create or buy a form to use and put the daily proceeds in an envelope. You will want to check your cash register receipts against what you actually have in your cash drawer to make sure it all matches at the end of each day.

Most accounting software will provide this type of report or you can do the report by hand. On the next page is an example of a daily sales tracking report.

> **TIP:** Balance your cash register float every day to your sales tracking report. (The "float" is the cash you start your day with in order to make change.)

Your Sales Pace

A good way to determine if your sales for the month are on track on any given day is to follow your sales pace. At any time during the month, this will tell you what you can expect to earn for the remainder of the month. Perhaps a big snowstorm has caused a sales slump for several days during the week. How much will you need to earn for the rest of the month to meet your revenue target?

The basic formula for calculating sales pace is:

Sales Pace = (Total Sales ÷ Number of Business Days so far for the month) x the number of business days in the month

From the Daily Sales Report (see next page), the store did $28,950 up to the 19th business day of the month. The sales pace is calculated using the preceding 18 days of sales as:

$$\$28,950 \div 18 \times 31 = \$1,608 \times 31 = \$49,858$$

Sample Daily Sales Report

Date: October 19, 20__

	Today	Month to Date
Cash	$1,319.10	$18,000.00
Checks	515.85	7,200.00
Master Card	180.04	2,400.00
Visa	$70.26	1,200.00
Other	0	400.00
Store Credit	0	0.00
Subtotal	**$2,085.25**	**$29,200.00**
Starting Float (Subtract)	(-250.00)	(-250.00)
Deposit Total	**$1,835.25**	**$28,950.00**
Returns	0	178.75
Voids	0	43.92
Pay Outs	0	250.00
Other	0	0
Total Cash Paid Out	**0**	**472.67**
Deposit Total Less Total Cash Paid Out	**$1,835.25**	**$28,477.33**
Sales Tax Collected	91.76	1,447.50
Cash Register Reading	$1,834.25	$28,477.65
Difference (+ or -)	$1.00	$0.32

So, for the entire month at the current sales pace, the store can expect around $49,858 in sales. If the store owner had projected $50,000 in sales for this month, then the sales pace is well on track. If the projection was $60,000, then sales are a bit behind.

Another point to consider is that sales on the 19th day of the month were above the average daily sales ($1,835 as compared to $1,608). The store owner can figure out now what the sales pace for the rest of the month will need to be to maintain the target pace.

Let's say the store owner had projected $60,000 in sales for the month. To calculate the sales pace that is needed for the remainder of the month, use the formula:

Sales pace = ($60,000 – ($1,608 x 18))/13 = $2,389

The store will need to produce $2,389 in sales each day for the remaining 12 days of the month in order to reach the $60,000 sales target for the month. Based on the preceding 19 days of sales, the store is a bit behind in its daily and month-to-date target sales.

Income Statement (Profit and Loss Statement)

Your income statement (also called a profit and loss or P&L statement) will tell you how much money you have in expenses and how much money you have in revenue for a given period. A number of things are necessary for an income statement.

You'll need to know:

- Your revenues for the period (gross sales minus returns and discounts)
- The cost of goods sold (what it cost you during the period to purchase merchandise for your store for the period)
- Your gross profit (revenues minus cost of goods sold)
- Your operating expenses (everything you must pay for to operate your store, including non-cash items like depreciation)

- Your net profit before and after taxes (revenues minus your operating expenses, and then subtract your tax liability)

The end result will tell you how much money your store is making — what is commonly referred to as "the bottom line."

You will want to decide which method of accounting you want to use, accrual method or cash method. In the accrual method, income is reported in the month it is earned and expenses reported in the month they are incurred (even if they have not yet been paid).

The cash method tracks actual money received and actual money spent. You do not consider any outstanding bills or invoices. The Business Owner's Toolkit website has an article entitled "Cash vs. Accrual Accounting" at **www.toolkit.cch.com/text/P06_1340.asp** that you can read as an introduction to this topic.

On the next page is an example of a typical income statement.

Cash Flow Statement

The cash flow statement allows you to quickly see whether more cash is coming in than going out, or vice versa, at the end of each month. It also allows you to make projections for certain periods of the year (such as the summer months when you might have increased sales due to larger numbers of tourists in your area at that time), or project cash flow year-over-year, and budget accordingly. You can also use it to track monthly cash flow and make projections for the coming month. This is handy if you're planning to make a large equipment or inventory purchase and need to know if you can afford it.

Cash flow is an important element of your financial picture. Monitoring cash flow lets you see how well your business is doing from day to day. Are you paying expenses with the money you take in from your operating revenues, or are you paying for expenses with other business funds such as banked working capital? If you are doing so with the former, your business is self-sustaining.

To keep track of expenses, you will need to keep copies of all receipts. This can be a challenge for new business owners who might have a habit of tossing out receipts for small items or not asking for receipts

Sample Income Statement

Income Statement [Company Name]
for month ending July 31, 20__

REVENUE ($)	
Cash sales	5,250
Credit card sales	1,600
Total Sales	**$6,850**

COST OF GOODS SOLD	
Inventory and material purchases	1,800
Shipping	50
Supplies	150
Total cost of goods sold	**$2,000**

GROSS PROFIT	$4,850

EXPENSES	
Lease	1,850
Insurance	75
Licenses & taxes	250
Office supplies & postage	100
Interest	95
Utilities	225
Wages	550
Telephone and Internet	115
Depreciation	55
Vehicle expenses	220
Repairs & maintenance	65
Total Expenses	**$3,040**

NET INCOME FOR THE MONTH	$1,810

in the first place. However, you are likely to have numerous small expenses related to your business, and these can add up over time. These expenses should be accounted for so you can minimize your taxes. And, of course, knowing exactly where your money is going will help you plan better and cut back on any unnecessary expenses. So make it a habit to ask for a receipt for every expense related to your business.

On the next page is a sample six-month cash flow worksheet for the first six months of operation.

Accounts Payable/Receivable Reports

Accounts payable are those accounts that you must pay — the money or bills your store owes. Accounts receivable are any accounts that are owed your store — the money that others owe you. Accounts receivable reports can vary widely depending on how you do business. For instance, accepting credit cards or selling over the Internet will affect how this report looks. And you may sell more at certain times than at others. If you have a layaway plan, this will affect your accounts receivable as well.

Accounts payable reports will tell you what bills you owe and when they are due. It's important to know clearly what you owe before you make any additional purchases. You have to be able to pay all your incoming bills and still have enough money for the other things you need to purchase for your business. An accounts payable report will help you to schedule when you will pay your bills, and will help you make sure nothing is neglected or forgotten.

Balance Sheet

A good metaphor for a balance sheet is that it is a snapshot, like a photograph, of your business taken at one moment in time. A balance sheet is the quickest way to see how your store is doing at a glance. It shows you what you own and what you owe. In other words, it is a balance of your assets against your liabilities.

The balance sheet consists of:

- Assets (the items you own including your inventory)

Sample 6-Months Cash Flow Worksheet

Month	1	2	3	4	5	6	Total
Starting Cash							
Cash Receipts							
Cash sales							
Layaways							
Credit card receipts							
Debit card receipts							
Total							
Cash Disbursements							
Start-up Costs							
Advertising							
Bank Charges							
Fees & Dues							
Fixed Assets							
Insurance							
Loans-Principal							
Loans-Interest							
Licenses & Taxes							
Purchases for resale							
Office supplies							
Professional fees							
Rent							
Repair & Maintenance							
Telephone & Internet							
Utilities							
Wages & Benefits							
Owner's Draw							
Monthly Surplus or Deficit (Cash less Disbursements)							
To Date Surplus or Deficit*							

** Monthly surplus/deficit to date is calculated by carrying through any deficit or surplus from month to month.*

- Liabilities (what you owe)
- Owner's Equity (what you've put into the business)

Types of assets are current assets and fixed assets (long-term and capital assets). A current asset is something that is acquired by your business over your business's fiscal year and will probably be used during that period to generate more revenue. Inventory, prepaid expenses such as rent already paid, and accounts receivable are examples of current assets. A fixed asset is an item that doesn't get used up quickly such as land, buildings, machinery, vehicles, long-term investments, etc., whose value is depreciated over time.

There are two types of liabilities: current and long-term. A current liability includes all those bills waiting for you to send a check out, such as utilities, short-term loans, or anything else payable within twelve months. A long-term liability is something that will be paid over a period of time longer than twelve months, for instance, a mortgage, a long-term equipment lease, or a long-term loan.

Owner's equity is anything you've personally contributed to (invested in) the business or any profit that remains in the owner's account that you have not drawn out in wages for yourself. If you used money from your personal accounts, or put your own assets into the business's inventory, the business "owes" you and it is recorded in this section of the balance sheet.

Here is what a typical balance sheet will look like. Note that assets balances exactly against liabilities + owner's equity. Also note that owner's equity equals assets minus liabilities.

5.4.3 Building Wealth

The following excellent advice on building wealth is adapted from the *FabJob Guide to Become a Coffee House Owner*, by Tom Hennessy.

Sometimes we get lost in the adventure of building a business and forget that on top of the perks of being our own boss, we can also make money in our venture However, like all things, success doesn't just happen—you have to create it.

Sample Balance Sheet

Balance Sheet [Company Name]
As of June 30, 20__

ASSETS	
Current Assets	
Cash	$12,200
Accounts Receivable	1,000
Inventory	80,000
Total current assets	**$93,200**
Fixed Assets	
Furniture	$3,500
Vehicle	20,000
Total fixed assets	**$23,500**
TOTAL ASSETS	**$116,700**

LIABILITIES	
Current Liabilities	
Accounts Payable	$5,000
Taxes Payable	2,225
Loan (short-term)	12,500
Current Portion of long-term debt	667
Total current liabilities	**$20,392**
Long-term Liabilities	
Loan	$35,000
TOTAL LIABILITIES	**$55,392**

OWNER'S EQUITY	
Capital – Owner's deposits	$90,000
Less Owner's withdrawals	(32,500)
Net Income/Loss	3,808
TOTAL OWNER'S EQUITY	**$61,308**

TOTAL LIABILITIES & OWNER'S EQUITY	**$116,700**

Even when you are making a good net profit each month, if you don't have a system for managing that profit, it can leak out during the course of a year. Then you will have nothing to show for your labor come New Year's Eve. In order to build wealth, you need to know how to squeeze all the value out of each and every dollar through budgeting, saving and investing.

Through these practices, you can build up a substantial amount of money without having a huge business. That is because time goes by very quickly. Five or ten years can slip away fast, and if you have a plan to carry you through those years, you will be amply rewarded. The two magic ingredients of time and compound interest are very valuable allies indeed.

Compound Interest and Debt

Think of compound interest as a steep hill. People are either on one side of this hill or the other. On one side of the hill, you have compound interest that you pay. On the other side is compound interest that is paid to you.

When you first start out in business, you generate a lot of debt. Your $200,000 loan may seem like a deal at 9 percent over 7 years, but is it really? By the time you pay off the loan, you will have paid an additional $70,295 in interest. That's over 35% of your loan.

When you are paying off your loan, you are looking up from the bottom of a steep slope towards the debt-free top. Most of the monthly payment is interest—hence the steepness. During the first year of the note, you have paid $21,486 in principal and $17,128 in interest. That is a lot of interest compared to principal. By the end of the note, this ratio will level off. In the final year, you will pay $36,795 in principal and only $1,818 in interest. At the top of the hill, you are debt free. You owe no interest and you receive no interest.

A business can't really move to the other side of the hill and receive interest because the government punishes businesses that retain profits by taxing them. You need to spend money on capital improvements or pay it out in wages or other forms of compensation, again triggering taxes. A good accountant will help you to minimize paying taxes while maximizing compensation.

Paying Off Debt

Accountants don't like businesses to pay off debt too fast because it creates phantom income. This is because you can only expense interest, not principal since you never really owned the principal in the first place. It wasn't your money; you borrowed it.

When you wrote that loan payment check every month, the principal you paid back wasn't yours in the first place so it is not considered a legitimate expense. Only the interest that you pay on that loan payment is considered yours and therefore you are allowed to expense that portion of the payment.

In the example earlier, you paid $21,486 in principal and $17,128 in interest during your first year. You expense the interest on your income statement, but where does the principal go? You'll find it in the bottom line as profit. Only you gave that profit back to the lender and you get taxed on it, even though you don't actually have the cash anymore. That is why it is called phantom income. A good accountant can help you deal with this issue and at the same time help you to pay down your loan quicker and minimize taxes on phantom income.

If you can pay off your loan in 5 years instead of 7 years, you can save $21,197 in interest payments. That is significant. To generate the cash to do this, though, you need to learn the value of money.

Here is a good math lesson for you and your employees. Let's assume that you are netting 8% profit before taxes. Every time you spend money on expense items, that is money that normally would go straight to the bottom line in the form of net profit (except you spent it).

Suppose you bought a box of mechanical pencils for $9.95 at the office supply store. How much in the way of sales do you need in order to produce enough profit to pay for them? The easiest way to figure it out is to divide $9.95 by your net profit percentage, which is 8%.

$$\$9.95 \div .08 = \$124.37$$

Looking at it another way, on $124.37 you would generate net profit of $9.95, which is 8% ($124.37 x .08).

You need to sell an additional $124.37 in merchandise to produce enough profit to cover your pencil purchase. Every time you spend a dollar, a corresponding sale is needed to pay for it. That's over an above your regular sales. You'll need to generate an additional $124.37 above your usual sales in order to pay for your pencils.

Thinking about the value of a dollar in these terms can have a drastic effect on your bottom line. When you think about the amount of related sales needed to offset expenses, you'll consider your purchases more carefully.

Forced Savings Account

In a forced savings account, you automatically transfer a specific amount of money from your checking account into an interest-bearing account on a certain day of each month. It follows the old rule "Pay yourself first." If you don't do this, the year will slip by and you will have nothing to show at the end of it for all your efforts.

Even $100 a month is easy to do for most businesses. At the end of the year you will have $1,200 plus interest to do whatever you like with. Use it to pay for a vacation, employee bonus, or a new piece of equipment (that you didn't have to borrow the money for, saving even more money in paid interest).

Your bank can set this up for you. Your interest is better if your money is invested in treasury securities. Talk to a stockbroker or investment advisor about different options. For example, $2,000 per month invested in an index fund averaging 10% per year will grow to $412,227 in 10 years. At the same time, you want your money invested in something safe, but you want it to be accessible in case you need to write a check for some emergency.

There is nothing wrong with creating wealth. It is only through profit that you provide capital to grow your business and pay wages. You're taking responsibility for your own financial well being. As you save and invest, you start to live on the other side of the interest hill and you start earning money without actually having to work for it. It's a beautiful thing to watch.

5.5 Employees

5.5.1 When to Hire Help

Even if you plan to start on a shoestring budget, chances are you will need at least one other employee to help during busy times (weekends, especially), or to give you a day off here and there.

Many business owners prefer to work all the hours their store is open, closing shop a couple of days a week, during holidays and for vacations. This system can work very well, especially if you notify your customers in advance of vacation time so they aren't disappointed with a wasted trip. You can even use the reminder as a selling tool by including a coupon for them to use when you return from vacation.

However, most shop owners reach a point in their careers where they want to make more profit by staying open more days or hours, or the store is so busy on a daily basis that they need the extra help at all times. In addition, malls and downtown business areas may have strict rules or bylaws about operating hours, and they'll fine you if you don't comply. You may not want to be in the store all the hours that it is required to be open, so you'll need to hire someone to be there when you're not.

Many retailers these days have a rule that if there are ever more than three people in line at the express checkout, then they will open another line. You might want to adopt this "three's a crowd" policy, too. If you consistently have more than three people waiting for help, or to make a purchase, then you may need to hire.

Take a look at your finances and make sure you can afford another employee. Are you making enough profit to hire extra help on the weekends and holidays? Will it increase your profits even more? If customers are getting frustrated at the wait time and leaving, then it most definitely will. Perhaps your business has even grown to the point where you need a full-time employee.

There are several types of staff members you can hire, and each has its advantages and disadvantages. All employees should be considered as investments, since you will spend time and money hiring and training them. You will see a return on that investment in increased sales, higher productivity in your store, more free time for you, and even new ideas for running your store based on employee input.

Full-time staff members work 30 or more hours a week. Most people work only one full-time job at a time, so, since they spend so much of their week working with you, they will naturally develop a sense of loyalty to you. In addition, full-time employees become so familiar with your store's routines and procedures that they can assist in training new staff members and run things if you need to take a day off here and there. A particularly competent and loyal full-timer might even become your second-in-command as manager when you take a vacation or open your second location. Keep in mind that full-time employees also come with the extra burdens for you of increased paperwork, health and other benefits, employment insurance, and so on.

Part-time staff members generally work less than 30 hours a week. Many people work more than one part-time job, often because of the unavailability in certain industries for full-time opportunities. (As discussed above, full-time employees cost more to employ.) As a result, loyalty will be less assured from your part-time staff and they are more likely to leave you if they receive a higher-paying or full-time job offer from another employer. However, the advantage to you is that you will save money, time and paperwork by hiring part-timers.

Students, retirees, stay-at-home parents, or people who otherwise have flexible or irregular schedules make good candidates for part-time work. All of these potential staffers typically welcome the chance to earn some income without the demand on their time that a full-time job would have. However, you may find that they require more training, since they may not have worked in the retail industry before.

Temporary, casual or on-call help can also play an important role as staffers in your business. For example, you might offer a particular service in your store that needs only occasional attention, so you hire someone who specializes in that type of service to come in once a week or twice a month to perform it. Another source of temporary help is your own family members, who might occasionally assist with sales or other tasks, particularly during peak busy periods like holidays.

Many high school and college students are excellent ice cream shop employees as they enjoy the fun atmosphere and working part time. Plus, they tend to be available during peak work periods, such as after school and on weekends. Many of the shop owners we surveyed also reported how eager young people were to learn and how rewarding it was for them to help young people learn responsibility and develop work skills.

> *"I am very proud of my staff. I employ 25 kids ranging in age from 15-20. I hire them in very formidable years and have the pleasure of watching them grow into responsible, hardworking adults. The transformation from their first year to their last is incredible. Most of them come to Capannari's not knowing how to hold a broom...by their last year they have headed committees that allowed them to create an event, schedule, inventory, purchase, implement and evaluate that event's ROI. We empower our young kids to take initiative and implement their ideas. They invest in our philosophy and thrive in those possibilities. I love it."*
>
> — Katie Dolan Dix, owner, Capannari Ice Cream

No matter which type of employees you decide to hire, start small. Hire a part-timer to get a feel for being an employer. If you like the person you hired and they're working out well, you might want to offer them increased hours or even a full-time position. If you hire someone on a full-time basis in the beginning and find that you can't afford to keep them on full-time, you will likely loose that employee and generate hard feelings. Hiring someone part-time also gives you the flexibility to hire someone else if the person you originally hired doesn't work out.

5.5.2 Recruiting Staff

Hiring employees can be one of the most challenging aspects of owning a business. It can be difficult to find an employee who learns easily, is friendly with your customers, is honest, and comes to work on time.

Qualities of Great Employees

Have you ever gone into a store and been treated rudely or without concern by an employee? Everyone has run into a rude salesperson at some time or another. Sometimes store salespeople are so rude and so unconcerned that potential customers leave the store without buying something they fully intended to purchase. A rude employee can hurt your sales and cost you customers.

But if you pick the right employees, you will have other people who care about your store and the customers who come there, and who will work to make your store a success. So it is vital that you choose carefully.

As you think about the demands of your new store, the niche you are hoping to fill in your community and the customers you hope to have, make a list of the qualities you want in your employees. Think about the type of people who will be easy for you to work with, who will be warm and helpful to the customers, and who will be an asset to your store.

Consider some of the following qualities of great retail employees:

- Honest
- Hardworking
- Responsible
- Reliable
- Friendly
- Knowledgeable
- Polite
- Good sales ability
- Good customer service ability
- Niche experience (e.g. employees with experience working in restaurants)

Now that you know the kind of people you want, you have to find them. If you talk about your store — and you should, because it's a good way to generate excitement — you can ask everyone you come into contact with if they know someone who would be a good employee for your store. Your regular customers are a good source for referrals, and more than one store owner has hired a customer to work as an employee in their store. Almost everyone knows someone who is looking for a job — it never hurts to ask around.

Advertising

The first place to advertise your job openings is in your own store. You can put a "Help Wanted" sign in the front window, and another by the cash register. Also consider posting your ad with your local high school or college. Many have Job Openings boards or offer job-hunting assistance to students.

Another option is placing an ad in your local paper's employment classifieds. Depending on the job market in your community, this can be an excellent way to find good local employees. Make sure your ad is eye-catching and uses just a few words to get the right kind of people through your door. Consider the following ad:

LOOKING FOR A FUN PLACE TO WORK?

> YoDazzles on Riverfront Commons is looking for bright, part-time servers to join our team. Do you have a great smile and enjoy people? Do you love helping people? Ice cream or foodservice experience a plus. Great working environment. Come in to fill out an application today. 1099 Riverfront Dr., Holidaytown.

Make sure the ad gets the point across quickly. Classified advertising is expensive and is priced by the word. Therefore, it is important to get your point across as quickly as you can. The ad above is about 60 words long.

Make sure all the vital information is included. Potential applicants need to know where to apply. In the above ad, the owner prefers that applicants come to the store to fill out an application and intentionally does not give a phone number. Because the store is often staffed by only one person, phone calls can be disruptive to service. Also, in order to save you lots of time with applicant questions, remember to include the basics about the job in your ad, including any benefits. One important thing to mention is whether the opportunity is full-time or part-time.

Make sure your ad is correct before it runs in the paper. When you work with an ad rep from your local paper, always ask them to give you a copy of your classified ad as it will appear, so you can check for mistakes. When your ad appears, check it again and make sure it is correct — especially your contact information.

Make sure that you include words or phrases that quickly help potential applicants find themselves in your ad. In the example advertisement above, the title includes the important word "fun." Potential applicants who don't really like boisterous or active environments will know immediately that the job isn't for them, and people who do like to work in energetic places will be drawn to read on and perhaps come in to fill out an application.

When you run an ad, decide ahead of time if you are too busy for phone calls and would prefer the first round of submissions to be sent by fax or email. Taking prescreening phone calls from applicants is time consuming. Decide what works best for you and your hiring schedule.

5.5.3 The Hiring Process

The selection process starts with the prospective employee filling out an application. Here are some other things to look out for when prospective employees come in to fill out an application or drop off a resume:

- Are they dressed nicely? Well-groomed?
- Are they polite or do they say, "Gimme an application"?
- Are they alone? Chances are that if the potential employee can't come to fill out an application without their best friend, they can't work without their friends either.
- What does your gut instinct tell you?

The Interview Process

The purpose of an interview is to get to know potential applicants as much as you can in a short period of time. It is therefore important that most of that time be spent getting the applicants to talk about themselves. Most employers with limited interviewing experience spend too much time talking about the job or their store. And while that is certainly important, it won't help you figure out to whom you are talking and if that person is a good match for your store. A good rule of thumb to follow is that the applicant should do 80% of the talking.

To make the best use of your time, have a list of questions prepared in advance. This will keep the process consistent between applicants. You can always add questions that pop up based on their answers as you go along. Possible questions to ask include:

- Why did you apply to work here?
- What is the ideal schedule you would like to work?
- When can you absolutely not work?
- What sort of experience do you have that you feel qualifies you for this job?
- Tell me about your last job and why you left.
- What was the best job you ever had-the one you had the most fun in?
- Who was your best boss and what made them so great?
- If I talked to someone who worked with you, what would they say about your work habits?
- Do you have any ambitions in this business? If not, what would be your perfect job?

To get a sense of how an employee will actually behave on the job, it is also a good idea to ask "behavioral questions." Behavioral questions ask applicants to give answers based on their past behavior. An example is "Tell me about a time you had to deal with a difficult customer. What was the situation and how did you handle it?" Instead of giving hypothetical answers of what someone would do in a particular situation, the applicant must give examples of what they actually have done. While people's behavior can change, past performance is a better indicator of someone's future behavior than hypothetical answers.

You can also ask questions that communicate your store policies to discover if the applicant will have any issues in these areas. Some examples are:

- When you are working, I expect your full attention to be on my customers. I do not allow private phone calls unless it is an emergency. Is that a problem?

- It is important that we open on time. I expect my workers to be punctual. Is there anything that could keep you from being on time for every shift?

By being clear on specifics and details in the interview, you can hash out any potential problems right then and there or agree to go your own ways because it is not going to work.

Discussing Pay

Another area to be clear about is what the pay is. Some employers will tell you not to talk money until you make the actual job offer, but that is really your choice. You do not want to go through the interview process, agonize over your decision, choose Johnny Good, offer the job and find out he does not want it because he thought it paid more and included health and dental benefits.

The government establishes a minimum wage that workers must be paid. Whether or not you want to pay over this amount is up to you. However, if you want the best candidates, then you'll need to offer them a competitive salary. Ask around — find out what other retail stores in your area are paying. To learn more about minimum wages in your area check out the U.S. Department of Labor website at **www.dol.gov/esa/minwage/america.htm**.

For wage information in a variety of occupations in Canada, visit the Services Canada website at **www.labourmarketinformation.ca** (click on "English", and then choose "Wages & Salaries" in the left frame menu). Visit **www.hrmanagement.gc.ca/gol/hrmanagement/site.nsf/en/hr11110.html** for Employment Standards in Canada, including information about minimum wage.

Employees are paid either weekly, bi-weekly, or on the 15th and last day of each month. You should have sufficient funds in your business checking account to ensure payroll checks will be covered. You may offer employees direct deposit paychecks (in which their pay is deposited into their bank accounts) or regular checks (which they may take to the bank themselves). Ask your accountant to set up a payroll for your store and maintain it for you. That way, you can be assured that you are making the correct amount of deductions for taxes and other benefits.

References

Once you have found an applicant who appears to be a good fit, you can learn more by checking their references. The best references are former employers. (Former co-workers may be friends who will give glowing references no matter how well the employee performed.)

Many companies will not give you detailed information about a past employee. They are only required to give you employment dates and sometimes they will confirm salary. But many times you will be able to learn a lot about a potential applicant from a reference phone call. A good employee is often remembered fondly and even asked about by a former employer. An employer may not be able to tell you much about a bad employee for liability reasons, but they can answer the question "Is this employee eligible to be rehired?" Here are some other additional questions from Tom Hennessy, author of the *FabJob Guide to Become a Coffee House Owner*:

- How long did this person work for you (this establishes the accuracy of their applications)?
- How well did they get along with everyone (looking for team skills)?
- Did they take direction well (code words for "did they do their job")?
- Could they work independently (or did they sit around waiting to be told what to do next)?
- How did they handle stressful situations (this is important, especially if you are busy)?

If the references make you feel comfortable, call the employee to let them know they have a job and to come in and fill out the paperwork.

5.5.4 New Employees

After you shake hands and say, "The job is yours!", you have to know how to work with the new employee to make sure it is a positive experience for everyone.

New Employee Paperwork

When a new employee is hired there will be paperwork they must fill out. In the U.S. this will be a W-4 and an I-9 form. In Canada, the employee will give you their social insurance number; you must also have them fill out a TD1. The U.S. W-4 and Canadian TD1 are legal documents that will determine the amount of tax that is to be deducted from an employee's wages. The U.S. W-4 and Canadian T-4 forms are legal documents verifying how many tax deductions a new employee has. The amount of tax you will withhold as an employer varies based on the amount of deductions that an employee has. Have the employee fill out the forms, and then file them in a folder labeled with their name which you will keep on file.

Check with your state or province's labor office to make sure you are clear about all the forms employees must fill out to work. The sites below give more information on legal paperwork, including where to get blank copies of the forms your employees will need to fill out.

- *SmartLegalForms.com*
  Sells blank forms on CD
  www.hrlawinfo.com/index.asp

- *GovDocs Products - Employee Records and Personnel Forms*
  Sells blank forms by the pack
  www.hrdocs.com/Posters/hrproducts/

- *Canada Revenue Agency*
  Download and print any form you need.
  www.cra-arc.gc.ca/forms/

Employee Emergency Contact Card

If the unexpected happens, as it sometimes will, you want to be prepared. Having employees fill out an emergency card for their file will help you contact their doctor, spouse, or other friends or family members in case of an emergency. Besides being the most rational and human thing to do, being prepared in this way can safeguard you against liability.

Make sure every employee's emergency card contains the following:

- Their correct and updated address and phone number
- Their family doctor and choice of hospital
- Any medications taken
- Allergies or special medical conditions
- The name and phone number of a family member emergency contact
- The name and phone number of an alternate emergency contact

Make sure that the emergency cards for staff, including one for you, are filled out and placed in alphabetical order in a filing cabinet or another location, and that everyone who works with you knows where this information is kept. Ask employees to verify that their emergency information is correct and updated as soon as it changes.

New Employee Orientation

Showing up on the first day of a new job is stressful for any employee. The new employees you hire are full of hope and anxiety, and are trying their best to make a good impression and be successful in your eyes. You should do your best to make them feel welcome and appreciated. Here are some tips to help them succeed:

- Make definite orientation plans for your new employee. Develop a list of what you will show and tell your employee, and go through each point. (This is where it helps to have a procedures manual as described in section 6.1.)
- Plan for the employee to have lunch with you or a friendly co-worker on the first day.
- Don't expect your brand new employee to be able to do everything on the first day. Realize that the first few days in your store will be a time for your new employee to learn and become comfortable with procedures.
- Don't throw your new employee into the fire. Starting them out on the day of the biggest sale in your store's history is a bad idea. Choose a time that is relatively slow-paced to let your new employee learn in a calm environment.

- Once your employee has been working for a few days, schedule an informal meeting to check in. Ask them to voice questions, comments, and possible concerns. Offer some positive feedback about your new employee's performance.

Taking the time to make sure your new employee feels comfortable and positive working in your store will pay off in the long run. Happy employees who feel positive about what they are doing often become long-term assets for your business.

Training, Motivating, and Retaining

It costs less to retain the staff you have than to recruit and train new staff, so make sure you keep open lines of communication with your employees. Take the time to ask them how things are going. Listen intently to what they say. Perhaps they are spending more time in your shop than you are and can offer valuable insight to problems you might not have noticed.

Encourage, and if you can, pay for staff to take courses to help them be the best they can be at their jobs. This not only helps them feel good about themselves, but will solidify their attachment to you and your business.

Think of interesting ways to motivate your sales staff. Could you offer a discount on items? An incentive bonus for hitting a sales target? Find out what motivates them, and create a sales incentive program that suits them.

Stay Informed

The government has many laws that protect workers in the workplace. It is important to be aware of these laws and to make sure that your store abides by them. The U.S. and Canadian governments have websites that provide information on almost any issue concerning employment law. Make sure to check how these laws affect your store and how you can abide by them. The U.S. Department of Labor website is located at **www.dol.gov**. In Canada, you'll find employment law information at the Human Resources and Skills Development Canada website at **www.hrsdc.gc.ca**.

6. Getting and Keeping Customers

6.1 Marketing Your Business

Assuming you have a good location, you will get some foot traffic off the street. People will walk into your store out of curiosity and some of them will buy from you. While this walk-in business can certainly contribute to your success, you can achieve even greater success by attracting customers to your store through effective marketing.

If your store is located in a shopping mall, the mall administration will have a calendar of promotional events that you can participate in. Likewise, if you have a store in a popular shopping district, there will likely be a local merchants association that you can join for cooperative advertising and events. In addition to any marketing you do through your mall or merchants association, you will likely need to do additional promotion on your own. This section outlines a variety of techniques you can try.

"One thing I wish I had known before I became an ice cream shop owner is that you need to do a lot of outside events in order to be successful. The outside events help to generate the revenue you will need to keep going during the slower months."

—Pam Nardinelli, owner, Marble Slab Creamery

6.1.1 Advertising

There are many places you can advertise your store, including the Yellow Pages, newspapers, magazines, radio, television, and the Internet. It is wise to combine two or more of these media, but you will want to consider several factors before you decide for sure which you choose. You'll want to know how much a particular advertisement costs, how long it will last, and most importantly, what consumers it will reach.

Cost

Your advertising dollars go towards supporting the media organization you're buying an ad from. The more expensive the media, the more expensive its ads are likely to be. A high-school yearbook will be able to offer much lower rates than a daily newspaper, and a college radio station (if it takes ads at all) will be cheaper than the area's hottest new music station. And television ads are the most expensive of all.

To find out how much various ad types cost in your area, call your local media outlets and ask them to send you a rate card. Rate cards list all the advertising options offered by the media outlet, and they often include other useful information such as demographic statistics (age, gender, income level, etc.) about the target audience — the type of viewers, listeners, or readers the outlet tends to reach.

Before you make any decisions, read the rate card and target audience information carefully. Is this the media outlet where most of your customers will hear your message? Sixty percent of your advertising budget should be aimed at existing customers, so keep that in mind when you're looking at the rate cards.

If advertising in a local magazine is really inexpensive, but you know most of your customers prefer to listen to the radio, you might want to try the magazine ad as an experiment to see what kind of new customers you might get from it. On the other hand, if you know your customers read the local daily newspaper, you should plan on doing most of your advertising there, and perhaps even forego the expensive television ad that targets people unlikely to shop at your store.

Yellow Pages

Yellow Pages ads can help you attract people from outside of your immediate area, particularly if you have a unique niche. Take a look at Yellow Pages ads for other retail stores like yours to get ideas (look under categories that match your type of business).

You can either design the ad yourself, have the Yellow Pages design it for you, or hire a designer. If you are interested in advertising, contact your local Yellow Pages to speak with a sales rep. Check the print version of your phone book for contact information. To find the Yellow Pages online, go to **www.yellowpages.com** (U.S.) or **www.yellowpages.ca** (Canada).

Newspapers and Magazines

Consider specialty magazines for your area that pertain to your store's niche. (Most communities have free newspapers or magazines directed at specific audiences.) Read a magazine or newspaper carefully to see if an advertisement for your store would fit with the theme of the paper, the articles, and the other ads.

Also consider advertising in newspapers with classified ads for merchandise like yours. These might be known locally as a bargain, trader, or shopper newspaper. For example, one major advertising newspaper in the U.S. is **www.traderonline.com**, and a similar paper in Canada is **www.buysell.com**.

Many publications will provide you with a free media kit with lots of information about their readership. This information will help you determine if their readers are the sort of customers you are looking for and if it is the right publication for your ad. Some publications will design your ad for free, while others will design it for an additional cost and give you a copy of the ad that you can then run in other publications if you wish.

Creating Effective Ads

Some people spend years learning how to create the most effective ads. Since we do not have years, we're going to focus on a couple of key points. For additional tips on creating effective ads read the article entitled "How to Run Effective Advertisements" at **www.usatoday.com/money/smallbusiness/ask/2001-07-30-ask-ad.htm**.

Most people need to see an advertisement several times before they buy, so running an ad only once may not give you as much business as you hope. A small ad that you run every week for a couple of months can generate more business than a single full page ad.

You can test a variety of ads, relatively inexpensively, by buying local ads on Google at **http://adwords.google.com**. Try different offers and wording to see which ones are most effective. You can set a maximum daily spending limit which keeps your costs down if lots of people click on your ad without buying. The offers that result in sales might also be effective in your other advertising as well.

One of the most effective ways to draw people into your store – and to test the effectiveness of each ad – is with some sort of incentive. An incentive can be anything from a discount coupon to a free sample.

To measure advertising effectiveness with coupons, it's a good idea to put a time limit or expiration date on it. Make sure this date is clearly printed on the coupon. It should allow customers enough time to get themselves to your store – maybe a week or two – but not so much time that they forget about the coupon, thinking they can use it well into the future. Tie the coupon to a date that's easy to remember, such as the end of the month.

The coupon offer should be simple, but with high perceived value — a buy one, get one free offer, or perhaps "This coupon good for 30 percent off your entire purchase," or "Redeem this coupon for a free waffle cone with your ice cream purchase." Above all, it should require that customers come into your shop to redeem their coupons. The idea is to get them to pay you a visit, see what other things you have for sale, and maybe buy something besides what they came for with the coupon.

6.1.2 Free Publicity

One of the best ways to market — with potentially excellent results for minimal cost — is to get free media publicity. While you don't have the final say over what gets reported, the exposure can give a boost to your business.

Public Service Announcements

If you are working with a charity, you may be able to get a Public Service Announcement aired on local radio stations. Write a 15 second or 30 second announcement and send it to "Public Service Announcements" at local radio stations. It probably will not be prime time, during the drive home, but every bit of exposure helps. Also, contact your local cable company to find out how to submit Public Service Announcements to the community channel.

Press Releases

Another way to get free publicity in local newspapers or magazines is by using a press release. Press releases typically announce an event. They should be a page or less, encompass the main points, and be put together as though they were going to be printed verbatim in the newspaper (they sometimes are). A sample press release appears below. You can find additional tips at **www.publicityinsider.com/release.asp** and **www.xpresspress.com/PRnotes.html**.

While you can self-promote, you do need to tie it into the community somehow. Try to brainstorm ways your activity benefits the community. If you donate to charity, then this should be an easy tie-in for you.

Donations

Donations are a good way to get your shop's name and products into the public eye. You'll probably be approached for donations by churches, community centers, non-profit or not-for-profit organizations, schools, sports teams, and more. They might ask for a cash donation but, more often, will want a product (such as an ice cream cake) that they can use as a prize in a raffle or drawing.

Sample Press Release

FOR IMMEDIATE RELEASE Date: April 16, 2010

CONTACT:
Ima Yogurtseller
YoDazzle
1099 Riverfront Dr.
Holidaytown, SC 29444
Phone: XXX-XXXX
Website: www.yodazzle.com

FROZEN YOGURT SHOP OPENING
ON RIVERFRONT COMMONS

YoDazzle announces the arrival of frozen yogurt to Holidaytown and invites everyone to join them in its grand opening celebration on May 1. YoDazzle will be offering premium nonfat frozen yogurt with an assortment of dazzles, or delectable toppings. Join them at 1099 Riverfront Drive, on the east side of the Riverfront Commons. The grand opening will start at 11 a.m. with a visit from H'town's hometown actor, Jason Depp, now starring in Pirates of the Bahama Triangle. The first 100 customers will receive a free medium yogurt with the topping of their choice. The next 100 customers will receive a free small yogurt with the topping of their choice. Raffles for free yogurt and special discounts will be held throughout the day. Be sure to enter for the grand prize: A free yogurt once a week for a year. Festivities will last until closing at 11 pm.

Yo Dazzle is owned by Ima Yogurtseller, and co-managed by Iluva Treat. It will be open from 11 am to 11 pm every day.

You don't, by any means, need to donate to every organization that asks. But ones that offer charitable tax receipts are worth considering, as are causes you believe in. Ones that you know will reach a large number of people are always worth supporting, because you'll have your shop name recognized by a large group of people as a donor. Be sure to ask for acknowledgment in any programs or posters made for the event.

When donating, it is nice to donate a flashy item that will catch the eyes of those who will see it. But consider donating coupons or gift certificates instead – something that will bring people into your store to collect their free item– and possibly encourage them to buy something else or prompt a repeat visit.

6.1.3 Promotional Tools

When you start a new business you will have to invest in some business promotional tools at the outset. These tools should be designed in a way that promotes both your business and the style of your business. Fonts on business cards, letterhead, ink colors, and even your advertising should all be designed to reinforce that style.

If you have a computer with a high quality laser or ink jet printer, you may be able to inexpensively print professional looking materials from your own computer. Free templates for all the print materials you are likely to need in your business can be found online.

HP offers templates for a variety of programs at **www.hp.com/sbso/productivity/office**. For example, you can create a matching set of stationery (business cards, letterhead, envelopes) in Microsoft Word or a presentation in PowerPoint. The site includes free online classes and how-to guides to help you design your own marketing materials.

Another excellent resource is the Microsoft Office Online Templates Homepage at **http://office.microsoft.com/en-us/templates**. At this site you can search a database to find templates for:

- Business stationery (envelopes, faxes, labels, letters, memos, etc.)
- Marketing materials (brochures, flyers, newsletters, postcards, etc.)
- Other business documents (expense reports, invoices, receipts, time sheets, etc.)

Business Cards

Business cards are a definite must in any business. A business card gives customers the essential contact information for your store, and every time you hand one out you should think of it as a mini-advertisement.

The cost of business cards can vary depending on how much or how little of the work you do creating them. You can make your own business cards if you own or have access to a computer. Office supply stores sell sheets of cards that come with perforated edges to go through any type of printer.

You can also hire a graphic artist to design a logo, do the layout and even arrange for printing. Most print shops have a design specialist on staff to help with these facets as well. Whichever way you decide to go, make sure the style of your card is in sync with the style you are promoting in your business.

When ordering your cards from a printer, the more you order the less expensive they are. When you order 500 cards, for example, the cost is minimal, generally around $50 to $65 depending on how many colors you have on your card and the card stock you use. Shop around to see where you can get the best deal.

Another alternative when you're just starting out is to use free business cards from VistaPrint.com. You can order 250 cards from them, using a variety of contemporary designs, and you only pay for shipping. The only catch is that they print their company logo on the back. If you don't mind having their logo on the back of your business cards, this is very economical. If you prefer not to have another company's name printed on the back of your business cards you can order 250 cards for about $20 plus shipping from VistaPrint without their logo.

Brochures

Having an attractive, catchy brochure is a good marketing tool especially when you go out to local business or other events; and you can also send your brochure to the media. Brochures give people a snapshot of what your business is all about. When coming up with a brochure, a graphic artist can help you design and lay it out. They also work closely with printers and know who is good and can do it in a timely matter for a good price.

The cost for printing brochures can range from a few hundred dollars (for one color on simple cardstock) or a few thousand dollars if you opt for color and glossy paper. Spend time on the copy and layout designs of your brochure and enlist the help of a professional designer if necessary.

Many printers will have an in-house design department who can do the artwork for you, but make sure you have a hand in developing the text. You are the best-qualified person to describe what your business is all about. Also, check for any typos in your phone number, email address or other contact information or you will be paying the printer to fix 1,000 brochures or doing it by hand.

You can use software such as Microsoft Publisher to design and print your own brochures, or you could try an online brochure-making service where you create the design from a template, such as Vistaprint (**www.vistaprint.com/brochures/gallery.aspx**). For a truly professional look you should enlist a service such as VistaPrint or a printer in your area to do it for you. Look in the Yellow Pages under "Printers."

While the challenge of designing an effective brochure is one thing, how to effectively distribute them is another. Brochures have an advantage over business cards in that they can sit in an office or a waiting room and will be picked up and read by the people waiting. Try to find places to leave them where people reading them might appreciate knowing about your store. Brochures can also be distributed by mail or handed out in conjunction with or instead of a business card.

Flyers

Flyers, also known as one-sheets, are essentially a brochure without the fold. They can be colorful and contain graphics, but often do not, making them more cost effective. A run of 250 one-sheets will cost very little, and the option to create these at home with a decent printer is also there.

Many of the tips mentioned for creating an effective brochure apply to one-sheets. Again, pay special attention to your contact information and make sure that it is correct.

One-sheets can be handed out at conventions and association meetings. Attaching a business card to your one-sheet is also a good strategy. You can also hang them in local grocery stores; ask to leave some out at the library, post them in laundromats and anywhere else your target market hangs out.

Printers

Brochures and one-sheets can be easily designed, paid for and delivered without leaving the house, using one of several on-line graphics companies. Here are a few you might want to consider:

- *FedEx Office*
  www.fedex.com/us/officeprint/main/

- *Acecomp Plus*
  www.acecomp.com/printing_brochures.asp

- *The Paper Mill Store*
  www.thepapermillstore.com

- *VistaPrint*
  www.vistaprint.com

6.1.4 Your Website

A website is an excellent tool for any retail store owner. It lets people know what you do, who you are, how to contact you, and where you are located. Your website can also complement your other marketing efforts. Let people who come into your store know you have a website, and mention your web address in every piece of advertising or written material you create about your store.

Ideas for Your Website

The basic structure of your website should include the following:

- Home page to navigate through your site
- Menu items with photos
- "About Us" page: this is where you let your customers know who you are and what expertise you have
- Contact information with your store hours, address, phone number, fax number, and perhaps directions or a map

Here are some features and additional information to consider including on your own store's website:

- A photograph of the front of your store
- Information about parking around your store
- Gift certificate information
- Your email contact information
- Articles related to your business, such as fun facts about ice cream

Developing a Website

If you are already experienced at creating web pages, or learn quickly, you can design your website yourself using a program such as Microsoft's Front Page or a free program like SeaMonkey (available at **www.seamonkey-project.org**. Otherwise, it's a good idea to hire a web designer through word of mouth or the Yellow Pages. Of course you should visit sample sites they have created before hiring them.

You may be able to put up free web pages through your Internet Service Provider (the company that gives you access to the Internet). To present a professional image and make your web address easier for clients to remember, consider getting your own domain name, such as www.yourstorename.com.

To present a professional image and make your web address easier for customers to remember, consider getting your own domain name, such as www.yourstorename.com. There are a number of sites where you can search for and register a domain name. One web host we have found that provides good service for a low cost is **www.godaddy.com**. Microsoft also offers a quick search for domain name availability using their sign-up feature at **http://smallbusiness.officelive.com**. (They'll also help you to set up a free website for your business.)

If your preferred domain name is available, but you're not yet ready with your website, you can also "park" your domain. This means that you register the domain so that someone else does not take it before you're up and running with your business website. You then park the domain with your web host.

> **TIP:** Do not use a free web hosting service unless you don't mind having your customers see pop-up ads for products unrelated to your store!

Promoting Your Site

No matter how much you spend on creating your website, if people don't know it exists, it won't help your business. Make certain you list your site on all your business forms, cards, and brochures. Encourage people to visit your site by mentioning it as often as you can, for example, whenever you write an article, give a presentation, or are interviewed by the media.

Make sure people can find your website by getting it into the search engines and listing it with industry websites. While some sites and search engines charge a fee to guarantee that your website will be included in their directory, you can submit your website for free to Google at **www.google.com/intl/en/submit_content.html**. Once you're on Google, your site is likely to be found by other search engines as well.

Your web hosting company may offer a search engine submission service for an additional fee. You can find information about "optimizing" your website, to help it rank higher on search engines, at the Search Engine Watch website at **http://searchenginewatch.com** and at Google's Webmaster Help Center at **www.google.com/support/webmasters**.

In addition to the free search engine listings, you can advertise on the search engines. See section 6.1.1 for more information.

Photography for Your Website

Digital cameras are now within the budgets of most people, and using them has taken the hassle out of developing film and then scanning them into a digital format in order to show your items to your online visitors.

Points to consider for photographs on your website:

- Make sure the subject is well lit but not washed out and not underexposed. Often, taking the shot in the daylight is your best bet. You might find the need to buy a box for photographing small merchandise in order to make your pictures look their best.
- You only need images of 72 dpi (dots per inch) for the web as opposed to the higher resolutions needed for printing of 260 to 300 dpi. It's important that, if you intend to use the same pictures for a brochure or any printed item, you shoot the picture at the highest resolution possible. Failing to do so will mean grainy printed pictures and an overloaded website.

6.1.5 Networking

Perhaps the best way to spread the word about your business is through other people. When you open your store, make sure you get the word out to your family and friends. Consider sending a postcard, and inviting them to your store's opening. You can also build your clientele by getting to know members of local clubs and by attending as many functions as possible to network with others who might help your business grow.

Chamber of Commerce and Visitors Bureaus

Often the local Chamber of Commerce and tourism groups, such as convention and visitors bureaus, are instrumental in getting the work out that you've opened a new business in town. Joining a group like the Chamber or visitors bureaus usually costs money, but the benefits, which include networking opportunities, educational seminars, and much more, is worth the investment for many business owners.

To find out how to contact your local chamber, visit the national websites. For the U.S. Chamber of Commerce visit **www.uschamber.com/chambers/directory/default.htm**. For the Canadian Chamber of Commerce Directory visit **www.chamber.ca/index.php/en/links/C57**. You can find convention and visitors bureaus on the on the United States Directory of Local Chambers of Commerce & Visitor Bureaus website at **www.2chambers.com** (click on the link to the Convention and Visitors Bureau for your state).

Word-of-Mouth

It's time to get your customers working for you. If you can develop a personal connection between you (that is, your business) and your customers they will be your best sales tools. What they say is worth more than hundreds of expensive ads.

One person telling another that your store is the best place to get wonderful ice cream is money in the bank. But how do you get to that point? By being everything your customers expect, honest, hardworking, fun to be around, knowledgeable, and—it's worth repeating—honest.

> **TIP:** Ask special customers to write brief reviews of your store and services. Add these "testimonials" to your newsletter, brochures, and ads.

"Our most effective marketing tool has been our ability to create an atmosphere where people feel they are part of our family and our experience. So many people have watched our growth and feel a part of our successes. These customers tell others about us and invite them to join the 'experience.' Word of mouth has been huge and generated at a grassroots level."

— Katie Dolan Dix, owner, Capannari Ice Cream

Cultivate Referrals

You can find additional customers by cultivating referrals. To do this, get to know your customers by chatting with them when they're in your store. Don't be afraid to ask them if they know of anyone who could use your products and services. Ask them to refer that person to your store.

Of course, the best way to get your customers referring business to you from others is to offer them the best possible customer service. In the next section, we'll offer some customer service tips that will keep your customers happy and get them talking about your store to others.

6.1.6 Your Grand Opening

Holding a grand opening can be a great way to introduce yourself and your new business to potential customers. If planned carefully, such an event can make your target market aware of your presence in a big way. The goal is to generate curiosity and interest in your business, as well as to make people aware of how you differ from the competition. If you're taking over an existing business you may want to let people know that the business is under new ownership and let them know how you plan to keep existing customers happy and serve the needs of new customers.

If you are opening a franchise operation (as explained in section 3.2.2), your franchisor actually may require you to hold a grand opening. Usually they will provide you with guidance as to how they would like it to be conducted. Also, your franchisor may require you to have a certain amount of available capital on hand in order to pay for the event. For information about holding a grand opening for a franchise, you should consult with your franchisor. In this section, we will look at how a non-franchise business owner can host a grand opening event.

Some of the elements to consider when planning your grand opening are:

- *Budget:* How much money can you put toward the event?
- *Timing:* When is the best time to reach the most people?
- *Publicity:* How do you make people interested in attending your grand opening?
- *Invited guests:* Who can help to attract people to your event (local celebrities, for example)?
- *Advertising:* What are the best ways to get the message out to your target market?
- *Promotions:* How will you reward people for attending?

Budget Considerations

There are a number of factors you should consider when planning your grand opening budget. First, you should put aside a certain amount of money in your start-up budget (see section 3.4.2 for more about start-up financial planning) for the event. Whether your start-up capital comes from your own cash resources or a loan, your plan for a grand opening should be clearly stated in your business planning documents.

Some grand opening budget items include extra staffing, advertising, printing invitations, brochure or flyers, buying promotional items, hiring a master of ceremonies, hiring a remote local radio broadcast from your store, hiring a guest speaker or celebrity look-alike, hiring a D.J. or band, hiring a caterer to supply refreshments, etc. You should find out the costs for all of these things well in advance and then figure out how much of your start-up cash you can devote to each.

Timing Considerations

When to hold your grand opening is also a major consideration. If you are in a downtown location, then the best time to hold your grand opening might be through the week when traffic is high in the area. If you are opening in a mall or strip mall, then the best time might be on the weekend when these are busiest.

Another consideration is the season. You shouldn't plan a grand opening close to any major holidays, since people are too busy to give much attention to a new store opening. Worse, many people travel during holiday times and this can have a negative impact, too. Although that can work for you if you're opening during a peak tourist season in a tourist-oriented location.

Time of day is important, also. According to one Chamber of Commerce source, the best time of day for a grand opening is from Tuesday through Friday, from 10:00 a.m. to 12:00 p.m., because this is the best time to get media attention and maximize attendance. You can informally survey local businesses where you plan to open to determine the highest traffic periods in that area.

Publicity and Advertising Considerations

There are a number of ways to get publicity for your event. You might want to consider a press release; distributing brochures, flyers or menus; contacting your local radio or television station to ask them to do an interview with you; paying for a remote on-location broadcast and so on. Earlier sections in this chapter have great advice on how to generate publicity and tips for effective advertising.

Promotional Considerations

In promoting your grand opening, you'll want to give people a reason to attend. Put yourself in the place of your hoped-for clientele and answer for them the question: "What's in it for me if I attend?" The answer might be something like a 10-20% discount on products or services, a free sampling of your services, free refreshments (some businesses offer coffee and doughnuts or a barbecue), gift merchandise (giveaways) and so on. The chance to meet a highly regarded celebrity can also be an incentive.

Invited Guests

Who you invite to your grand opening can also have an impact on attendance. You might want to have the mayor or other high-profile citizen cut the ribbon to officially open your business. Perhaps you know someone famous who wouldn't mind helping out for the event.

Another consideration is to invite people who have a wide network of contacts. They can help to spread the word about your business. Other people to invite include:

- Local Chamber of Commerce members
- City or town council members
- Other government officials
- Local business owners
- Any contractors who worked on remodeling your store
- Business Improvement Area representatives and members
- Any other person or group who you know has a wide sphere of influence

6.1.7 Other Marketing Ideas

There are a lot of unique ways to get the word out about your store. While you can and should use traditional methods of advertising, keep

A Sample Grand Opening Plan

Grand Opening Budget

Extra staff (4 hours)	$100.00
Master of Ceremonies	$500.00
Advertising Costs	$600.00
Printing Costs	$450.00
Catering service	$500.00
Balloons	$50.00
Ribbon	$30.00
Remote on-location radio broadcast	$500.00
Giveaways (at cost)	$200.00
Total Grand Opening Costs	**$2,930.00**

Schedule

9:00 a.m.	Meet with staff and go over the plan
9:15 a.m.	Start setting up, local radio crew to arrive to set up for on-location broadcast
9:30 a.m.	Refreshments ready to go
9:45 a.m.	Master of Ceremonies and Mayor to arrive
10:00 a.m.	Invited guests to arrive; greet guests and the public in front of the store
10:15 a.m.	Mayor to cut ribbon; invite guests and public inside
10:20 a.m.	Refreshments to be served
10:20-11:30 a.m.	Meet and greet; interviews with local radio talent
11:30-11:50 a.m.	Hold draws for door prizes
11:50 a.m.	Thank everyone for coming. Final words from M.C.
12:00 a.m.	Start clean-up

your mind open to new and exciting ideas as well, because you never know when you might stumble upon one that will be a huge success.

Here are some additional ideas you may want to try to market your business:

- Hold an Open House
- Unveil new menu items (e.g. special flavors during holidays)
- Taste fairs
- Ask your customers to tell others about the store. Give them a small gift or a discount coupon for bringing in a friend.
- Work with other complementary businesses. Put your fliers in their store and theirs in yours. Do promotions with them.
- Hold a contest. For example, you could have a prize drawing or give an award to the person who comes into your shop dressed in the craziest outfit you have ever seen. (You might even get some media coverage out of it.)
- Print and wear T-shirts or baseball hats with your store's name and logo. Give them out to your best customers.
- Paint your shop logo on your car.
- Post your business card on every bulletin board you see.
- Have a Birthday club and give participants a free item on their birthdays.
- Have an events calendar posted on your website and in your store. List special promotions, such as Flavor of the Week, and sales.
- Have a frequent shopper card or offer specials such as 10 percent off one day a month to customers on your mailing list.

"Community involvement is the third most important factor in Capannari Ice Cream's success...second only to our product and customer service. We have built our brand around our involvement in the community and we attribute it to a major part of who we are. It is extremely important that wherever

your shop is that you not only invest in your business but that you invest in the community around you. You need to be a responsible business person within your business and within your community."

— Katie Dolan Dix, director, National Ice Cream Retailers Association

6.2 Customer Service

As you saw in the previous section, many ideas for marketing your store involve encouraging your customers to return to your store.

An even more important factor in getting repeat business is excellent customer service. Exceeding your customers' expectations is a sure way to keep them coming back to your store for years to come. In this section we will discuss several suggestions for you to follow in order to better serve your clientele.

6.2.1 Greeting Customers

Most customers behave similarly when they walk into a small retail store. First, they want a greeting just to know someone is there. Second, they might be cautious for the first few minutes, hoping no one will pounce on them with a high pressure sales pitch. To set customers at ease, you should keep the chit-chat light at first. They'll soon start to loosen up and then you could ask what they are looking for.

Consider using this four-step approach to greeting customers effectively:

Step #1: When customers enter the store, greet them. Say, "Hello. How are you?" Smile, smile, smile. Never, ever ignore your customers. Assume the store is like your home and the customers are your neighbors coming in for a visit.

Step #2: Pause for a minute and then start some chit-chat. "Isn't it a beautiful day outside?" or "I like your necklace." Keep it positive and upbeat. Don't say, "Don't you hate this lousy weather we're having?"

Step #3: Next, ask if they need help. "Can I help you?" "Are you looking for something specific?"

Step #4: If customers look uncertain or are having difficulty making a selection, ask if they would like to sample a product (when possible). Keep sample spoons and small paper cups for taste tests by the service counter.

Customers do not like feeling pressured. However, they also do not like feeling ignored. We've all been in stores where staff members are busy chatting and joking with each other and ignoring customers, or they're on the phone with a personal call, too busy to be disturbed by a customer. Even if your store is busy with several customers at once, make sure you at least acknowledge the person when they first come in and let them know that you're around to offer your help if needed.

> *"The personal attribute that has helped me the most as an ice cream shop owner has been my ability to make every customer feel special. Smiles, samples and a welcoming environment will keep your customers coming back."*
>
> — Pam Nardinelli, owner, Marble Slab Creamery

Greeting Regular Customers by Name

You will need a good memory to pull this one off, but writing down a description of the person and some details can jog your memory. You may not remember every single person who comes into your store, but you should make an effort to get to know the regulars.

There are a few visualization techniques you can use to recall someone's name. There are a couple of articles you can read online that will help you with this skill. The first, "How to Remember Names When You Meet People" (**www.learnthat.com/courses/lifestyle/names**) is a short article that offers some easy memory devices like repetition and word association to use in order to remember names. The second, "How to Remember Names" at **http://ezinearticles.com/?How-To-Remember-Names&id=470003** is a little more in-depth, and expands on some of the concepts in the first article. In addition, the article introduces devices like mnemonics and "cluster imprinting" for recalling people's names.

TIP: Another way to show customers they are important is to focus on them. If you are working with a customer and the phone rings, allow the machine to pick it up. You can return the call as soon as you are finished with the customer who is in the store.

6.2.2 Making the Sale

Here are some ways to help you identify what customers want so you can make the sale.

Making Contact

Treat each customer as if he or she is your best customer. Get to know what customers want, and be patient while they make up their mind. It's always best to be subtle. Being pressured by a talkative salesperson the minute they step into a store is a sure-fire way to have customers scurrying back out to the street. Most people who frequent ice cream shops want some time to browse before determining their selection.

Qualifying Customers

Qualifying a customer means finding out what the customer wants. Find out how much they are willing to spend. Ask questions that lead to a conversation, not just elicit a yes or no response. Get them to talk about what they're looking for.

If a customer has objections to buying, you need to listen carefully to why that person isn't buying. Are your prices too high? Are they looking for a menu item other than one you're currently offering? Hopefully you will be able to save the sale, but this might be a good time to scrutinize your menu items and prices to see if you need to make some changes.

Courting the Customer

Relationships of all types require work. Be very careful when you're subtly trying to find out what customers want and why they aren't buying that you don't overstep that line of comfort that most people need to keep salespeople at arm's length. They want to feel in control of the situation, and if you push too hard their discomfort will mount and they'll probably run out the door.

How do you know if you've gone too far? Answers to your questions will become clipped; customer's will avoid your eyes, and begin to move closer to the door. Re-establishing a level of trust might be quite difficult at this point, so it is probably best to be as friendly as possible, apologize, and offer them room to continue to look at their leisure.

Some shoppers would rather browse in silence and you'll become quite adept at figuring out who they are the minute they walk into your store. They will be courteous, and return your greeting, but perhaps only smile tightly if you offer any further conversation. The best idea is to just let them be; they probably know what they want and are enjoying themselves.

Closing the Sale

The best salespeople know the art of closing the sale. If you're lucky, the customer will be the one who asks for what he or she wants. If not, it's time for you to go to work on the sale. This might be one of the most difficult parts of running your business.

You might want to just sit back and let your wonderful atmosphere and fabulous merchandise do the selling for you. While that's a great position to be in, many people like to hang on to their hard-earned cash and need that extra push to place an order.

Ask for the sale. Say, for example, "What can I get for you?" With time you'll find your own rhythm and know just when and how to prompt a hesitant customer.

> *"The industry has become much more competitive in the last three years. Quick service restaurants continue to expand their frozen treat offerings and supermarkets have significantly expanded their ice cream selections. As such the retail store owner must provide outstanding personalized service to build a loyal customer base. In addition community involvement is becoming a must to own your local store marketing area."*
>
> — Gary Bales, president, Carvel Corporation

6.2.3 Getting Repeat Business

If you set up shop in a busy neighborhood, you may have a steady stream of customers and not need to do anything to attract them. However, if you want to maximize your sales, consider taking a more proactive approach to identify your customers and keep them coming back.

Giving Customers What They Want

To give customers what they want, you need to know something about them. While the amount of customer information you keep in a customer database is entirely up to you, try to keep as much information as your software program allows.

Here are a few of the things you might want to keep track of:

- Customer preferences
- Buying patterns
- Special interests

You will probably at least want regular customers' mailing information and some of their preferences listed. Once you know your customers' interests and preferences, you can make suggestions.

Suggesting items that you think will suit the customer can show you're interested in the customer themselves — not just a sale. Take the time to work with your clients and find out what their needs and desires are. Ask your customers what they want, whether it's something you currently carry or not (you could even include a brief survey in your email newsletter). Then create a wish list in a note book and keep it up-to-date.

Once you have been in business for a while, you will have a few regular customers who shop from you year round. Pay attention to their likes and dislikes and track them. If you get something in that you know they would love, pick up the phone and give them a call. Again, this is excellent customer service. You will more than likely make additional sales as well, because they will likely buy several things while they're in picking up the new item that you have put aside for them.

These extra touches and consultations can keep customers coming back again and again.

Dealing with Difficult Customers

One of the best ways to deal with difficult customers is to gather as much information as you can. Let's use an example. Perhaps you have a customer who consistently buys items and then finds fault with them. You suspect that she is purchasing items to try out and then asking for her money back because she didn't like the item as much as she had thought and wishes she had ordered something else, but you do not really have any proof of this.

The customer comes into your store once again, orders an item, then complains that it tastes funny. You ask what was wrong with the item. Do not immediately close your ears because you think you know the answer. Really listen to what she has to say; practice those listening skills we just discussed.

Asking customers for feedback can help you determine what the real issue is (they may not know what different items taste like, for example) and this may help you develop solutions that improve customer relations and save you costs. In this case, offering the customer a sample before a purchase will help her to determine whether an item meets her taste requirements and will make her feel like a treasured customer at the same time.

Knowing what the real issues are can help you change your operating procedures also. Perhaps many customers are sending an item back.

If so, check to see what it tastes like. There may be a problem with the freshness or quality of the product.

Customer Surveys

Feedback can also help you keep your good customers coming back. Each time a person buys an item, ask them to take the time to complete a survey, which will include the types of items they like to collect, or have an affinity for. Keep survey sheets near your cash register and also have a survey on your website.

Be careful, though, because privacy laws are very specific, and you need to ensure you customers that you won't be sharing the information you collect and how you will be using it.

Sample Customer Survey

Name: ______________________________

Address: ______________________________

____

Phone: ______________________________

Email: ______________________________

Any particular item(s) you are interested in acquiring? Please describe your wish list.

____

____

____

____

____

Can *[Store Name]* send you newsletters about events and special promotions? ❑ Yes ❑ No

Please note: [Store Name] will only use your information to provide better services to you; your information will not be shared.

TIP: By offering an incentive, such as a prize (perhaps a gift certificate or discount coupon), you will find people are more inclined to fill out your survey. Let them know that this way, if you get something in they may love, they will be the first to know.

Sorting through the contacts you make this way might seem time-consuming, but setting up a database, either by a simple listing in a spreadsheet, which you can sort and search, or using a database program, is the key to making sure you use the information you have taken the time to collect.

Set up your system to be able to search categories that match your customers' wish lists against new items you get in; for example, a simple category listing that then expands to the various types in that category that they are interested in.

You might want to rate which customers to contact first, perhaps by how well they pay or by how often they have been in the store. Let them know they are preferred customers.

Conclusion

We wish you all the best in your future endeavors and offer you the following advice and reflections from our ice cream shop experts as you prepare for the next step in your new venture.

> "Come into this industry with open eyes and expectations, work hard and you can build a fun and profitable business."
>
> — Gary Bales, president,
> Carvel Corporation

> "For those getting into the business, my advice is to create a good product but to also focus on the atmosphere and the philosophy of your company. If you are an honest, hardworking business owner that focuses on running a company with integrity you will exude these qualities to the public. People respond to the companies that truly are invested in them and the community they live in. Make your product, your staff and your customer the most important priority in your business."
>
> — Katie Dolan Dix, owner,
> Capannari Ice Cream

> "The most rewarding aspect of a career as an ice cream shop owner has been providing customers with the best ice cream on earth! When people come for ice cream they are usually celebrating something. Whether it is a good grade or learning to ride a bike, we can enhance the moment with good customer service and great ice cream. The smiles on ice cream eaters' faces is the most rewarding thing to me!"
>
> — Pam Nardinelli, owner,
> Marble Slab Creamery

> "Don't give up. It's very hard work and it takes time to build a business. It doesn't happen over night, while we would like it to, so you must stick with it to achieve the maximum toward your goals. There is the pot of gold at the end of the rainbow. Not necessarily filled with real gold, but with the fulfillment of having a great job, being able to have quality time with family and helping young people to learn responsibility while they are working for you. Having some gold in the pot at the end helps."
>
> — Irene Macones,
> longtime Carvel franchisee